Harmony Out of Discord

Reuniting a Splintered World

Copyright © 2024 by RK Books

All rights reserved.

No part of this publication may be reproduced, distributed, or transmitted in any form or by any means, including photocopying, recording, or other electronic or mechanical methods, without the prior written permission of the publisher, except in the case of brief quotations embodied in critical reviews and certain other noncommercial uses permitted by copyright law.

This book is a work of fiction. Names, characters, places, and incidents are products of the author's imagination or are used fictitiously. Any resemblance to actual events, locales, or persons, living or dead, is entirely coincidental.

ISBN: 978-969-479-224-8   E-Book

ISBN: 978-969-479-225-5   Paper-Back

ISBN: 978-969-479-226-2   Hard-Back

Published by |

Table of Contents

Introduction 1

Chapter 1 Understanding Discord and Harmony 3

    Defining Discord and Harmony 3

    The Importance of Balance 6

    The Role of Conflict in Human Interaction 10

Chapter 2 The Origins of Discord: Historical Perspectives 14

    Ancient Conflicts: Seeds of Discord 14

    Wars and Revolutions: Catalysts of Division 17

    Colonialism and Its Legacy: Shaping Modern Discord 20

Chapter 3 Contemporary Discord: Exploring Global Divisions 24

    Political Polarization: Fragmentation in Governance 25

    Socioeconomic Disparities: Inequality Breeding Discord 28

    Cultural Clashes: Challenges to Global Harmony 31

Chapter 4 The Human Element: Psychology of Conflict and Harmony 34

    Understanding Human Nature: Instincts and Tendencies 35

    Cognitive Biases: Impediments to Harmony 37

    Empathy and Compassion: Building Blocks of Unity 40

Chapter 5 Communication Breakdown: Barriers to Harmony 44

    Miscommunication and Misunderstanding: Barriers to Harmony 45

    Language and Cultural Differences: Navigating Diversity in Communication 47

    Digital Disconnect: Challenges in Online Communication 49

Chapter 6 Bridging Divides: Strategies for Reconciliation 53

    Dialogue and Mediation: Paths to Resolution 54

Building Trust and Understanding: Keys to Conflict Resolution and Social Cohesion 57

Conflict Transformation: Turning Discord into Opportunity 60

Chapter 7 Cultural Unity: Celebrating Diversity in Harmony 65

Cultural Exchange and Appreciation: Fostering Understanding and Connection 66

Cultural Competence: Navigating Differences Respectfully 69

Fusion and Hybridization: Creating New Harmonies 72

Chapter 8 Political Unity: Building Consensus in a Polarized World 76

Finding Common Ground: Principles of Consensus Building 78

Political Reconciliation: Healing Divisions 81

Strengthening Democratic Institutions: Promoting Accountability, Participation, and Resilience 85

Chapter 9 Economic Harmony: Addressing Disparities and Inequality 89

Wealth Redistribution: Tackling Economic Disparities......................... 89

Inclusive Growth: Fostering Opportunities for All 93

Social Safety Nets: Ensuring Economic Stability................................... 97

Chapter 10 Environmental Reconciliation: Finding Balance with Nature 104

Conservation and Preservation Efforts: Sustaining Biodiversity and Ecosystem Health 104

Sustainable Development: Balancing Growth and Preservation 109

Climate Change Mitigation: Global Efforts for Environmental Harmony 113

Chapter 11 Technological Solutions: Tools for Unity in the Digital Age ... 119

Leveraging Technology for Connection 119

Digital Diplomacy: Online Platforms for Harmony 124

Artificial Intelligence for Conflict Resolution....................................... 128

Chapter 12 Education for Unity: Nurturing Harmony in Future Generations 134

Teaching Conflict Resolution Skills 134
Cultivating Empathy and Cultural Understanding in Schools............... 139
Promoting Global Citizenship Education 144

Introduction

In a world marked by deep divisions, where discord seems to echo louder than harmony, the pursuit of unity stands as a beacon of hope amidst the tumult. From ancient conflicts to modern-day divisions, humanity has grappled with discord in myriad forms, yet the quest for harmony remains an enduring aspiration. It is within this context that we embark on a journey to explore the intricate dynamics of discord and the profound significance of harmony in our collective existence. At its essence, discord represents the fracture of unity, the divergence of interests, beliefs, and aspirations that sow seeds of conflict and division. Whether manifested through political strife, cultural clashes, or socioeconomic disparities, discord permeates every facet of human interaction, shaping the course of history and the contours of contemporary society. Yet, juxtaposed against this backdrop of discord lies the enduring allure of harmony—a state of equilibrium, cohesion, and mutual understanding that transcends differences and fosters unity. The origins of discord trace back through the annals of history, woven into the fabric of ancient empires, medieval conflicts, and modern revolutions. From the conquests of empires to the struggles for independence, humanity's journey has been marked by periods of strife and upheaval, punctuated by fleeting moments of reconciliation and unity. Through the lens of history, we gain insight into the cyclical nature of discord and the transformative power of harmony to mend the fractures of the past. In the contemporary landscape, the specter of discord looms large, casting a shadow over global affairs and domestic politics alike. From the polarization of ideologies to the widening chasm of socioeconomic inequality, the challenges to harmony are manifold and multifaceted. Yet, amid the cacophony of discord, there exist opportunities for dialogue, understanding, and reconciliation—keys to unlocking the potential for a more unified and harmonious world. As we embark on this exploration of discord and harmony, we are called upon to confront the complexities of our shared humanity and embrace the imperative of unity in diversity. Through dialogue, empathy, and collective action, we can bridge the divides that threaten to tear us asunder and forge a path towards a future defined by harmony and understanding. In the pages that follow, we will delve deep into the intricacies of discord and the transformative power of harmony to transcend differences, heal wounds, and build a more just and equitable world. It is a journey that invites introspection, dialogue, and collective action—a journey towards reuniting a splintered world in the harmonious embrace of our shared humanity.

Chapter 1
Understanding Discord and Harmony

In the symphony of human existence, discord and harmony dance together, shaping the rhythm of our collective journey. Discord, the dissonant note that fractures unity and breeds conflict, stands in stark contrast to harmony, the harmonious chord that binds us together in mutual understanding and cooperation. In this inaugural chapter, we embark on a journey of exploration into the intricate dynamics of discord and the profound significance of harmony in our lives and societies.

At its core, discord represents the divergence of interests, beliefs, and aspirations that sow seeds of division and strife. It manifests in myriad forms, from the clash of ideologies to the fissures of inequality, permeating every facet of human interaction and shaping the course of history. Yet, amid the cacophony of discord, there exists the enduring allure of harmony—a state of equilibrium, cohesion, and mutual respect that transcends differences and fosters unity.

Through introspection and inquiry, we seek to unravel the complexities of discord and illuminate the pathways to harmony. By understanding the roots of discord and the mechanisms of harmony, we can navigate the turbulent waters of conflict and strive towards a future defined by cooperation, understanding, and peace. Join us as we embark on this journey of discovery, delving into the depths of discord and emerging with newfound insights into the transformative power of harmony.

Defining Discord and Harmony

In the intricate tapestry of human existence, few concepts are as fundamental and yet as elusive as discord and harmony. These twin forces, like opposing currents in a river, shape the ebb and flow of our lives and societies. To truly understand discord and harmony, we must delve deep into their essence, exploring their origins, manifestations, and implications for our collective journey.

The Nature of Discord

At its core, discord represents a state of disagreement, conflict, or disharmony. It arises from the divergence of interests, beliefs, and values among individuals or groups, leading to tension, strife, and often, outright confrontation. Discord can manifest in various forms, from interpersonal conflicts to geopolitical rivalries, each fueled by a complex interplay of factors ranging from ideological differences to competing interests.

One of the defining characteristics of discord is its disruptive nature. Like a discordant note in a symphony, it disrupts the harmonious flow of interactions, creating a sense of dissonance and discomfort. This disruption can have far-reaching consequences, fracturing relationships, destabilizing communities, and even sparking violence and conflict on a larger scale.

Moreover, discord is often accompanied by a breakdown in communication and understanding. As individuals or groups become entrenched in their positions, dialogue gives way to confrontation, empathy to animosity, and cooperation to competition. This breakdown in communication only serves to deepen the rifts between conflicting parties, perpetuating a cycle of discord and division.

The Roots of Discord

Understanding the roots of discord requires us to delve into the complex web of human psychology, sociology, and history. From a psychological perspective, discord can arise from a variety of factors, including differences in personality, values, and beliefs, as well as underlying emotions such as fear, anger, and resentment. Sociologically, discord often stems from inequalities in power, resources, and opportunities, as well as competing group identities and interests. Historically, discord has been a constant companion of human civilization, fueled by conflicts over territory, resources, religion, and ideology.

Indeed, throughout history, discord has been a driving force behind some of the most significant events and developments, from wars and revolutions to social movements and cultural shifts. Whether it be the clash of empires vying for dominance, the struggle for independence from colonial rule, or the ideological battles of the Cold War, discord has shaped the course of human history in profound ways.

The Elusive Quest for Harmony

In contrast to discord, harmony represents a state of agreement, cooperation, and mutual respect. It is characterized by a sense of unity, balance, and interconnectedness among individuals or groups, where differences are embraced rather than feared, and conflicts are resolved through dialogue and understanding.

Achieving harmony, however, is no easy task. It requires a commitment to empathy, tolerance, and compromise, as well as a willingness to transcend personal biases and prejudices. Moreover, it necessitates a recognition of the interconnectedness of all living beings and the realization that our actions have consequences that ripple far beyond ourselves.

Manifestations of Harmony

Harmony can manifest in various forms, from the harmonious coexistence of diverse cultures and religions within a society to the peaceful resolution of conflicts through dialogue and negotiation. It can be found in the rhythms of nature, where different species coexist in delicate balance, each playing its part in the larger ecosystem. It can also be experienced on a personal level, in moments of deep connection and understanding with others, or in the sense of inner peace that comes from aligning one's actions with one's values.

The Pursuit of Harmony

While the pursuit of harmony may seem idealistic in a world marked by discord and division, it is essential if we are to create a more peaceful, just, and sustainable future. This pursuit begins with each of us, in our daily interactions with others and the choices we make in our lives. It requires us to cultivate empathy, compassion, and understanding, and to actively seek out opportunities for dialogue and reconciliation.

Moreover, the pursuit of harmony necessitates systemic change at both the local and global levels. It requires us to address the root causes of discord, including inequalities in wealth and power, discrimination and prejudice, and environmental degradation. It also requires us to build institutions and systems that promote cooperation, justice, and sustainability, and to work towards a more equitable and inclusive world for all.

The concepts of discord and harmony are deeply intertwined in the fabric of human existence, shaping the course of history and the contours of contemporary society. While discord may seem omnipresent, harmony remains an enduring aspiration—a beacon of hope in a world marked by division and strife. By understanding the nature of discord and the elusive quest for harmony, we can begin to chart a course towards a more peaceful, just, and sustainable future for all.

The Importance of Balance

Balance is a concept that permeates every aspect of our lives, from the physical world around us to the inner workings of our minds and bodies. It is a state of equilibrium, harmony, and proportion that lies at the heart of well-being and flourishing. In this chapter, we will explore the multifaceted nature of balance, its importance in various domains of human existence, and the ways in which we can cultivate and maintain it in our lives.

The Physical World: The Dance of Balance

In the natural world, balance is a fundamental principle that governs the behavior of everything from atoms and molecules to planets and galaxies. It is the force that keeps celestial bodies in orbit, maintains the stability of ecosystems, and ensures the proper functioning of biological systems. Without balance, the delicate equilibrium of life would be upset, leading to chaos and disarray.

One of the most striking examples of balance in the physical world is the concept of homeostasis—the tendency of living organisms to maintain internal stability and equilibrium in the face of external changes. From regulating body temperature to balancing electrolytes and pH levels, homeostasis is essential for the survival and health of all living beings. It is a delicate dance of feedback mechanisms and physiological processes that ensure the body's internal environment remains stable and functional.

Moreover, balance is also crucial in the realm of ecology, where it governs the interactions between different species and their environments. Ecosystems are complex networks of relationships in which each organism plays a specific role, and the balance between predator and prey, producer and consumer, is essential for the health and resilience of the system as a whole. When this balance is disrupted—whether through human intervention, climate change, or other factors—it can have far-reaching consequences, leading to biodiversity loss, ecosystem collapse, and other negative outcomes.

The Mind and Body: Nurturing Inner Harmony

Just as balance is essential for the physical world, it is also crucial for the well-being of the mind and body. In the realm of psychology and mental health, balance is often equated with emotional equilibrium, mental stability, and psychological resilience. It is the ability to navigate life's ups and downs with grace and equanimity, remaining centered and grounded in the face of adversity.

One of the key components of mental balance is emotional regulation—the ability to recognize, understand, and manage one's emotions in a healthy and adaptive way. This involves being able to tolerate distressing emotions without becoming overwhelmed, as well as being able to express and communicate emotions effectively to others. When we are emotionally balanced, we are better able to cope with stress, build strong relationships, and navigate the challenges of life with resilience and confidence.

Moreover, balance is also essential for physical health and well-being. From maintaining a healthy diet and exercise routine to getting enough sleep and managing stress, there are many factors that contribute to physical balance. When these factors are in harmony, our bodies function optimally, and we experience greater energy, vitality, and overall well-being. However, when these factors are out of balance—whether due to poor lifestyle choices, chronic stress, or other factors—it can lead to a range of health problems, including obesity, heart disease, and mental health disorders.

Relationships and Social Dynamics: Finding Equilibrium

In the realm of human relationships and social dynamics, balance is essential for fostering connection, understanding, and cooperation. It is the ability to navigate the complexities of social interactions with grace and empathy, respecting the needs and boundaries of oneself and others while striving for mutual understanding and harmony.

One aspect of balance in relationships is the ability to maintain healthy boundaries—knowing when to say yes and when to say no, and being able to assert one's needs and preferences without infringing on the rights of others. This involves being able to communicate assertively, set limits, and negotiate conflicts in a constructive and respectful manner. When boundaries are too rigid or too porous, it can lead to problems such as codependency, resentment, and conflict in relationships.

Moreover, balance is also crucial for fostering empathy and understanding in our interactions with others. It is the ability to see things from multiple perspectives, empathize with others' experiences and emotions, and respond with compassion and kindness. When we are able to strike this balance, we build deeper connections with others, foster trust and intimacy, and create a sense of belonging and community.

Cultivating Balance: Practices for Well-being

Cultivating balance in our lives requires intention, effort, and commitment. It involves attending to our physical, mental, and emotional needs, as well as nurturing healthy relationships and social connections. There are many practices and strategies that can help us cultivate balance in our lives, including:

1. **Mindfulness meditation:** Practicing mindfulness can help us cultivate awareness of our thoughts, feelings, and bodily sensations, allowing us to respond to them with greater clarity and equanimity.

2. **Yoga and tai chi:** These ancient practices combine physical movement with breath awareness and meditation, promoting relaxation, flexibility, and inner peace.

3. **Self-care:** Taking time for ourselves to engage in activities that nourish and replenish us, whether it be reading a book, taking a bath, or spending time in nature.

4. **Setting boundaries:** Learning to assert our needs and boundaries in our relationships and interactions with others, and respecting the boundaries of others in return.

5. **Seeking support:** Asking for help and support from friends, family, or mental health professionals when needed, and offering support to others in return.

6. **Cultivating gratitude:** Practicing gratitude can help us shift our focus from what is lacking to what we have, fostering a sense of contentment and well-being.

By incorporating these practices into our daily lives, we can cultivate greater balance, resilience, and well-being, allowing us to navigate life's challenges with grace and equanimity.

Balance is a fundamental principle that underlies every aspect of human existence, from the physical world around us to the inner workings of our minds and bodies. It is essential for the health and well-being of individuals and societies alike, fostering harmony, resilience, and flourishing. By understanding the importance of balance and cultivating practices that promote it in our lives, we can create a more peaceful, healthy, and sustainable world for ourselves and future generations to come.

The Role of Conflict in Human Interaction

Conflict is an inevitable part of human existence, woven into the fabric of our relationships, societies, and history. While often viewed in a negative light, conflict serves a crucial role in shaping human interaction, fostering growth, innovation, and social change. In this chapter, we will explore the multifaceted nature of conflict, its underlying causes and dynamics, and its implications for individuals and societies.

Understanding Conflict

At its essence, conflict arises from the clash of interests, values, or goals between individuals or groups. It can manifest in various forms, from interpersonal disputes and family feuds to political rivalries and armed conflicts. Conflict is fueled by a complex interplay of factors, including differences in power, resources, identity, and ideology, as well as underlying emotions such as fear, anger, and resentment.

One of the key features of conflict is its dynamic nature—it is a process rather than a static event, evolving over time as the parties involved navigate their differences and seek resolution. Conflict often follows a predictable trajectory, beginning with the emergence of tension and disagreement, escalating into open confrontation or competition, and ultimately leading to some form of resolution or transformation.

The Functions of Conflict

While conflict is often viewed in a negative light, it serves several important functions in human interaction. One of the primary functions of conflict is to surface and address underlying tensions and grievances within individuals and societies. By bringing these tensions to the surface, conflict creates opportunities for dialogue, negotiation, and reconciliation, allowing individuals and groups to work through their differences and find common ground.

Moreover, conflict can also serve as a catalyst for growth and change, prompting individuals and societies to question existing norms, values, and power structures. It can spur innovation and creativity, leading to the development of new ideas, technologies, and social movements. In this way, conflict can be seen as a driving force behind progress and social transformation.

The Dynamics of Conflict

Conflict is characterized by a variety of dynamics and processes that shape its course and outcomes. One of the key dynamics of conflict is power—the unequal distribution of resources, authority, and influence among individuals or groups. Power imbalances can exacerbate conflict by creating conditions of oppression, exploitation, and injustice, leading to resentment and resistance among those who feel marginalized or disenfranchised.

Another important dynamic of conflict is communication—or, more often, the lack thereof. Poor communication can fuel misunderstandings, escalate tensions, and hinder efforts to resolve conflict constructively. Effective communication, on the other hand, is essential for building trust, fostering empathy, and finding mutually acceptable solutions to conflict.

Conflict Resolution Strategies

Resolving conflict requires a combination of skills, strategies, and processes aimed at addressing the underlying causes of conflict and finding mutually acceptable solutions. One approach to conflict resolution is negotiation, where the parties involved engage in a dialogue aimed at reaching a mutually beneficial agreement. Negotiation involves a range of tactics and techniques, including active listening, problem-solving, and compromise.

Mediation is another common approach to conflict resolution, where a neutral third party assists the parties involved in finding common ground and reaching a settlement. Mediation is often used in situations where the parties are unable to resolve their differences on their own or where there is a power imbalance that makes direct negotiation difficult.

In some cases, more formal mechanisms of conflict resolution may be necessary, such as arbitration or litigation. Arbitration involves the parties submitting their dispute to a neutral third party, who renders a binding decision based on the evidence presented. Litigation, on the other hand, involves resolving the conflict through the legal system, with a judge or jury ultimately deciding the outcome.

The Role of Conflict in Social Change

Conflict plays a central role in driving social change, challenging existing power structures, and advocating for justice and equality. Throughout history, social movements have emerged in response to perceived injustices and inequalities, mobilizing individuals and communities to challenge the status quo and demand change.

One of the most powerful examples of the role of conflict in social change is the civil rights movement in the United States, which challenged racial segregation and discrimination and ultimately led to the passage of landmark civil rights legislation. Similarly, the women's rights movement, the labor movement, and the LGBTQ rights movement have all used conflict as a tool for advancing their goals and promoting social justice.

Conflict is a complex and multifaceted phenomenon that shapes human interaction in profound ways. While often viewed in a negative light, conflict serves several important functions in society, including surfacing tensions and grievances, fostering growth and innovation, and driving social change. By understanding the dynamics of conflict and employing effective conflict resolution strategies, individuals and societies can navigate their differences and work towards a more just, peaceful, and equitable world.

Chapter 2
The Origins of Discord: Historical Perspectives

In the annals of human history, the origins of discord can be traced back to the earliest civilizations, where conflicts over resources, territory, and power laid the groundwork for millennia of strife and division. From the rise and fall of empires to the clash of cultures and ideologies, the pages of history are filled with tales of discord and conflict that have shaped the course of human civilization.

In this chapter, we will embark on a journey through time, exploring the origins of discord from ancient civilizations to modern times. We will delve into the dynamics of conflict in ancient Mesopotamia, the struggles for dominance among the great empires of antiquity, and the religious and ideological clashes that have defined much of human history.

By understanding the historical roots of discord, we can gain insight into the underlying factors that have fueled conflicts throughout the ages and the enduring impact they have had on the course of human events. Moreover, we can begin to appreciate the complexities of human nature and the challenges of navigating the tumultuous waters of history in our quest for peace and harmony.

Ancient Conflicts: Seeds of Discord

The dawn of human civilization was not merely a period of progress and innovation but also a time marked by profound conflicts and struggles. In this chapter, we delve into the ancient conflicts that sowed the seeds of discord, shaping the course of history and laying the foundation for the conflicts that would follow in later centuries. From the rise of city-states in Mesopotamia to the conquests of ancient empires, we explore the origins of conflict in the ancient world and its enduring impact on the trajectory of human civilization.

The Birth of Civilization and the Rise of City-States

The ancient world witnessed the emergence of some of the earliest civilizations, with Mesopotamia, Egypt, the Indus Valley, and China among the most notable. These civilizations were characterized by advanced agricultural practices, complex social hierarchies, and the development of writing systems and monumental architecture. However, they were also marked by intense competition and conflict among rival city-states vying for dominance and control over fertile lands and strategic resources.

In Mesopotamia, for example, the city-states of Sumer and Akkad engaged in frequent warfare, with conflicts arising over disputes over water rights, trade routes, and territorial expansion. The legendary city of Ur, with its powerful rulers and formidable army, often clashed with neighboring city-states such as Lagash and Uruk, leading to cycles of conquest, tribute, and rebellion.

The Rise of Empires and the Age of Conquest

As civilization advanced, so too did the scale and intensity of conflict. In the ancient Near East, the rise of empires such as Assyria, Babylon, and Persia ushered in an era of conquest and imperialism. These empires, with their vast armies and centralized bureaucracies, sought to expand their territories and exert control over rival states through military force and political dominance.

The Assyrian Empire, for example, was notorious for its ruthless military campaigns and brutal tactics, employing siege warfare, mass deportations, and scorched-earth policies to subdue its enemies. The Babylonian Empire, under the rule of Hammurabi, established one of the earliest legal codes, but it also engaged in conflicts with neighboring states such as Elam and Assyria, leading to periods of instability and upheaval.

Religious and Ideological Conflicts

In addition to conflicts over territory and power, the ancient world was also marked by religious and ideological clashes that fueled discord and division. From the polytheistic pantheons of Mesopotamia and Egypt to the monotheistic faiths of Judaism and Zoroastrianism, religious beliefs played a central role in shaping the identity and worldview of ancient societies.

In Mesopotamia, for example, the rivalry between the city-states of Babylon and Assyria was not only political but also religious, with each state vying for the favor of the gods and seeking to establish its supremacy over the other. Similarly, in ancient Egypt, conflicts often had religious undertones, with pharaohs invoking divine authority to justify their rule and legitimize their conquests.

Legacy of Ancient Conflicts

The ancient conflicts that shaped the course of history have left a lasting legacy that continues to reverberate in the modern world. The conquests of empires such as Assyria and Babylon laid the groundwork for the rise of later imperial powers, shaping the geopolitical landscape of the ancient Near East and influencing the course of world history for centuries to come.

Moreover, the religious and ideological conflicts of the ancient world have left an indelible mark on the cultural and intellectual heritage of humanity. The monotheistic faiths of Judaism, Christianity, and Islam, which emerged in the wake of ancient conflicts, have played a central role in shaping the moral and ethical values of Western civilization and the broader world.

The ancient conflicts that arose in the cradle of civilization laid the foundation for the tumultuous history of human society. From the rise of city-states to the conquests of empires, from religious rivalries to ideological clashes, these conflicts shaped the course of history and left a lasting legacy that continues to shape the world we live in today. By understanding the origins of ancient discord, we can gain insight into the complexities of human nature and the challenges of navigating the turbulent currents of history.

Wars and Revolutions: Catalysts of Division

Throughout history, wars and revolutions have been powerful catalysts of division, reshaping societies, redrawing borders, and altering the course of human events. From ancient battles fought with swords and spears to modern conflicts waged with tanks and drones, warfare has been a constant companion of human civilization. Similarly, revolutions—whether political, social, or cultural—have sparked upheaval and transformation, challenging existing power structures and fueling movements for change. In this chapter, we delve into the role of wars and revolutions as catalysts of division, exploring their causes, consequences, and enduring impact on the fabric of human society.

The Nature of Warfare

Warfare is as old as human civilization itself, with conflicts erupting over territory, resources, ideology, and power. From the ancient battles of Mesopotamia and Egypt to the global conflagrations of the 20th century, warfare has taken myriad forms, ranging from small-scale skirmishes to world-spanning conflicts that engulfed entire nations.

One of the defining features of warfare is its capacity to divide societies along lines of identity, allegiance, and ideology. In times of war, individuals and communities are often forced to choose sides, aligning themselves with one faction or another based on factors such as nationality, ethnicity, religion, or political affiliation. This division can lead to deep-seated animosities and resentments that endure long after the guns have fallen silent.

Wars of Conquest and Imperialism

Throughout history, wars of conquest and imperialism have been a driving force behind division and conflict. Empires such as Rome, Persia, and the Mongols expanded their territories through military conquest, subjugating neighboring peoples and imposing their will through force of arms. These conquests often resulted in the displacement of populations, the destruction of cultures, and the imposition of new political and social orders.

The European colonial empires of the 16th to 20th centuries further exacerbated divisions through their policies of exploitation, oppression, and cultural assimilation. Colonized peoples were subjected to violence, exploitation, and discrimination, leading to deep-seated resentment and resistance that fueled movements for independence and self-determination.

Revolutionary Upheaval

Revolutionary upheavals have also been powerful catalysts of division, sparking conflicts that pit old against new, tradition against progress, and authority against dissent. Revolutions such as the French Revolution, the Russian Revolution, and the Chinese Revolution overturned existing political orders, leading to periods of upheaval, violence, and social transformation.

These revolutions often pitted different factions against one another, including monarchists and republicans, conservatives and radicals, and capitalists and socialists. The resulting conflicts often tore societies apart, leading to civil wars, purges, and mass violence as competing factions vied for control and sought to impose their vision of the future.

Civil Wars and Internal Conflict

Civil wars and internal conflicts have been particularly divisive, tearing at the fabric of societies and pitting brother against brother, neighbor against neighbor. From the English Civil War to the American Civil War to the Spanish Civil War, these conflicts have been characterized by intense ideological, political, and social divisions that often result in widespread suffering and destruction.

Civil wars arise from a variety of factors, including ethnic and religious tensions, social inequality, and disputes over political power and representation. In many cases, these conflicts are exacerbated by external actors seeking to exploit divisions for their own gain, further fueling the cycle of violence and division.

The Legacy of War and Revolution

The legacy of wars and revolutions as catalysts of division is far-reaching and enduring. In addition to the immediate human cost in lives lost, infrastructure destroyed, and communities displaced, these conflicts leave lasting scars on the psyche of nations and peoples. They sow seeds of mistrust and animosity that can persist for generations, hindering efforts at reconciliation and healing.

Moreover, wars and revolutions often reshape the geopolitical landscape, redrawing borders, and redefining alliances in ways that can have far-reaching consequences. The aftermath of conflict is often marked by instability, insecurity, and the rise of authoritarian regimes that seek to exploit divisions for their own gain.

Conclusion, wars and revolutions have been powerful catalysts of division throughout history, shaping the course of human events and leaving a lasting impact on the fabric of society. Whether fought for conquest, independence, or ideological change, these conflicts have torn nations apart, divided communities, and sown seeds of discord that endure long after the guns have fallen silent. By understanding the nature of war and revolution as catalysts of division, we can gain insight into the complexities of human conflict and the challenges of building a more peaceful and just world.

Colonialism and Its Legacy: Shaping Modern Discord

The era of colonialism stands as a pivotal chapter in human history, marked by the conquest, exploitation, and domination of vast regions of the world by European powers. From the 15th to the 20th centuries, European colonial empires spanned the globe, reshaping societies, economies, and cultures in ways that continue to reverberate in the modern world. In this chapter, we explore the legacy of colonialism as a potent force shaping modern discord, examining its causes, consequences, and enduring impact on the fabric of human society.

The Age of Exploration and Expansion

The seeds of colonialism were sown in the Age of Exploration, as European powers embarked on voyages of discovery in search of new trade routes, wealth, and glory. The voyages of Christopher Columbus, Vasco da Gama, and Ferdinand Magellan opened up new worlds to European exploration and exploitation, leading to the establishment of trading outposts, colonies, and empires in distant lands.

The conquest of the Americas, Africa, Asia, and the Pacific brought European powers into contact with diverse peoples and cultures, setting the stage for centuries of conflict, exploitation, and domination. European powers such as Spain, Portugal, Britain, France, and the Netherlands competed for control over lucrative trade routes, natural resources, and strategic territories, leading to a period of imperial rivalry and expansion that reshaped the geopolitical landscape of the world.

The Mechanisms of Colonial Domination

Colonialism was characterized by a variety of mechanisms of domination, including military conquest, economic exploitation, and cultural assimilation. European powers employed a range of tactics to subjugate indigenous peoples and establish control over colonized territories, including warfare, coercion, and divide-and-rule strategies.

One of the primary goals of colonialism was economic exploitation, with European powers extracting natural resources, labor, and wealth from their colonies to fuel their own industrial economies. The establishment of plantation economies, mining operations, and cash-crop agriculture led to the exploitation and impoverishment of indigenous peoples, who were forced to work under harsh and often brutal conditions for the profit of colonial rulers.

The Legacy of Colonialism

The legacy of colonialism is complex and multifaceted, with far-reaching implications for the societies and peoples affected by it. On the one hand, colonialism brought significant material benefits to European powers, fueling economic growth, technological innovation, and the expansion of trade networks. However, these benefits came at a steep cost for the colonized peoples, who were subjected to exploitation, oppression, and cultural erasure.

One of the most enduring legacies of colonialism is the persistence of deep-seated inequalities between former colonizers and colonized peoples. The legacy of colonialism is still felt in many parts of the world today, with former colonies continuing to struggle with poverty, underdevelopment, and political instability long after gaining independence.

Cultural and Social Impacts

Colonialism also had profound cultural and social impacts on the societies it touched, leading to the disruption of traditional ways of life, the erosion of indigenous cultures and identities, and the imposition of European values and norms. The spread of Christianity, Western education, and European languages had a transformative effect on colonized peoples, reshaping their worldviews, beliefs, and social structures in ways that continue to shape their societies today.

Moreover, colonialism created deep divisions within colonized societies, pitting different ethnic, religious, and social groups against one another in the service of colonial rulers. These divisions often persist to this day, fueling ethnic conflicts, religious tensions, and social inequalities that undermine efforts at nation-building and reconciliation.

Contemporary Challenges

In the modern world, the legacy of colonialism continues to shape contemporary challenges and conflicts, from ethnic strife and political instability to economic inequality and social injustice. The effects of colonialism are evident in ongoing conflicts in regions such as Africa, the Middle East, and South Asia, where colonial borders, institutions, and power structures continue to influence the dynamics of conflict and division.

Moreover, the legacy of colonialism is also evident in the persistence of racism, discrimination, and social inequality in former colonial powers themselves, where colonial attitudes and structures continue to shape social relations and economic opportunities.

Colonialism stands as a potent force shaping modern discord, with far-reaching implications for the societies and peoples affected by it. From the conquest and exploitation of indigenous peoples to the imposition of European values and norms, colonialism has left a lasting legacy of division, inequality, and injustice that continues to reverberate in the modern world. By understanding the causes and consequences of colonialism, we can gain insight into the complexities of modern discord and the challenges of building a more just, equitable, and inclusive world.

Chapter 3
Contemporary Discord: Exploring Global Divisions

In the modern world, discord takes on new dimensions as globalization, technology, and interconnectedness bring societies closer together while simultaneously exposing and exacerbating divisions. From political polarization and economic inequality to cultural clashes and environmental degradation, contemporary discord manifests in a myriad of forms, shaping the dynamics of global politics, economics, and society.

In this chapter, we delve into the complexities of contemporary discord, exploring the underlying causes, manifestations, and consequences of global divisions. From the rise of populism and nationalism to the challenges of climate change and global migration, we examine the fault lines that divide nations and peoples, as well as the opportunities for dialogue, cooperation, and reconciliation.

By understanding the nature of contemporary discord and its implications for the future of humanity, we can begin to chart a course towards a more inclusive, sustainable, and harmonious world. Through dialogue, empathy, and collective action, we can confront the challenges of our time and build a future defined by cooperation, understanding, and peace.

Political Polarization: Fragmentation in Governance

Political polarization has become a defining feature of contemporary societies, shaping the landscape of governance and politics in countries around the world. Characterized by deep divisions along ideological, partisan, and cultural lines, political polarization has led to a breakdown in trust, cooperation, and compromise, resulting in gridlock, dysfunction, and fragmentation in governance. In this chapter, we explore the nature of political polarization, its underlying causes, and its implications for the functioning of democratic institutions and the health of civil society.

The Nature of Political Polarization

Political polarization refers to the divergence of political attitudes, beliefs, and preferences between different groups within a society. It manifests in various forms, including ideological polarization (e.g., liberal vs. conservative), partisan polarization (e.g., Democrat vs. Republican), and cultural polarization (e.g., urban vs. rural, cosmopolitan vs. nationalist).

At the heart of political polarization is the erosion of common ground and the rise of "us vs. them" dynamics, where individuals and groups view their political opponents as adversaries rather than fellow citizens with legitimate differences of opinion. This tribalism leads to the demonization of the other side, the dehumanization of political opponents, and the rejection of compromise and cooperation in favor of confrontation and conflict.

Causes of Political Polarization

Political polarization is driven by a complex interplay of factors, including social, economic, and technological forces that have reshaped the political landscape in recent decades. One key factor is the rise of identity politics, where individuals' political identities become intertwined with their social identities based on factors such as race, ethnicity, religion, and gender. This has led to the formation of political tribes, each with its own set of beliefs, values, and grievances.

Moreover, economic inequality and social stratification have contributed to political polarization by exacerbating divisions between rich and poor, urban and rural, and educated and non-educated segments of society. As economic disparities widen, so too do political attitudes, with marginalized groups feeling increasingly alienated and disenfranchised from the political process.

Technological advancements, particularly the rise of social media and online echo chambers, have also played a role in fueling political polarization by facilitating the spread of misinformation, conspiracy theories, and extremist ideologies. These platforms amplify voices at the fringes of the political spectrum, creating ideological bubbles where individuals are insulated from opposing viewpoints and are more susceptible to radicalization.

Implications for Governance

The fragmentation of governance resulting from political polarization poses significant challenges for the functioning of democratic institutions and the ability of governments to address pressing issues and challenges. In polarized political environments, cooperation and compromise become increasingly difficult as politicians prioritize partisan loyalty over the common good.

This gridlock and dysfunction can have far-reaching consequences, leading to legislative paralysis, government shutdowns, and a lack of meaningful progress on key policy issues. Moreover, the erosion of trust in democratic institutions and the political process undermines the legitimacy of elected leaders and institutions, further exacerbating divisions and undermining social cohesion.

Mitigating Political Polarization

Addressing political polarization requires a multi-faceted approach that tackles its root causes and fosters a culture of dialogue, empathy, and understanding. This includes efforts to reduce economic inequality, bridge social divides, and promote civic education and media literacy to counteract the spread of misinformation and conspiracy theories.

Moreover, political leaders must prioritize bipartisanship and compromise over partisan gamesmanship, working across the aisle to find common ground and advance the interests of all citizens. This may require electoral reforms, such as ranked-choice voting or nonpartisan redistricting, to reduce the influence of partisan gerrymandering and ensure fair representation for all voters.

Civil society also has a crucial role to play in mitigating political polarization by fostering spaces for constructive dialogue and engagement across ideological divides. Initiatives such as deliberative democracy forums, community organizing efforts, and interfaith dialogues can help build bridges between disparate groups and promote a sense of shared citizenship and common purpose.

Political polarization poses a significant threat to the functioning of democratic governance and the health of civil society. By deepening divisions, eroding trust, and fostering gridlock and dysfunction, political polarization undermines the ability of governments to address pressing issues and challenges facing society. However, by understanding the underlying causes of political polarization and implementing strategies to mitigate its effects, we can work towards building a more inclusive, resilient, and cohesive society where differences are respected, dialogue is valued, and cooperation is prioritized for the common good.

Socioeconomic Disparities: Inequality Breeding Discord

Socioeconomic disparities have long been a pervasive issue in societies around the world, creating deep divisions between the haves and the have-nots and exacerbating tensions along class, race, and gender lines. From widening income gaps and unequal access to education and healthcare to systemic discrimination and marginalization, socioeconomic inequality breeds discord by fueling resentment, alienation, and social unrest. In this chapter, we delve into the nature of socioeconomic disparities, their underlying causes, and their implications for social cohesion, economic stability, and political legitimacy.

The Nature of Socioeconomic Disparities

Socioeconomic disparities refer to differences in income, wealth, education, and opportunity that exist between different segments of society. These disparities can manifest in various forms, including income inequality, wealth concentration, and unequal access to essential services such as healthcare, education, and housing.

At the heart of socioeconomic disparities is the unequal distribution of resources and opportunities, which often perpetuates cycles of poverty and disadvantage across generations. Those born into poverty or marginalized communities face systemic barriers to social mobility, including limited access to quality education, employment opportunities, and social networks.

Causes of Socioeconomic Disparities

Socioeconomic disparities are driven by a complex interplay of structural, historical, and systemic factors that perpetuate inequality and injustice. One key factor is economic globalization, which has led to the outsourcing of jobs, the erosion of labor rights, and the concentration of wealth in the hands of a small elite. Globalization has also fueled the rise of precarious work, gig economies, and informal labor markets, exacerbating insecurity and instability for vulnerable workers.

Moreover, systemic discrimination and marginalization based on factors such as race, ethnicity, gender, and disability contribute to socioeconomic disparities by limiting opportunities and access to resources for marginalized groups. Structural inequalities in education, healthcare, and criminal justice further entrench disparities, perpetuating cycles of poverty and disadvantage across generations.

Implications for Social Cohesion

Socioeconomic disparities have profound implications for social cohesion, undermining trust, solidarity, and cooperation within societies. When large segments of the population feel marginalized, excluded, or left behind by economic growth and development, social tensions and resentments can boil over into social unrest, protest, and conflict.

Moreover, socioeconomic disparities can exacerbate divisions along lines of identity, exacerbating tensions between different racial, ethnic, and cultural groups. When inequality is perceived as unjust or illegitimate, it can lead to feelings of anger, resentment, and alienation, further deepening social divisions and eroding trust in institutions and authority.

Economic Stability and Political Legitimacy

Socioeconomic disparities also pose significant challenges for economic stability and political legitimacy, undermining the functioning of democratic institutions and the social contract between citizens and the state. When large segments of the population feel economically marginalized or excluded from the benefits of economic growth, they may lose faith in the political system and turn to alternative ideologies or movements that promise radical change.

Moreover, socioeconomic disparities can create fertile ground for populism, extremism, and authoritarianism, as disenfranchised groups seek scapegoats for their economic woes and turn to charismatic leaders who promise simple solutions to complex problems. This can lead to polarization, conflict, and instability, further undermining the stability and legitimacy of democratic governance.

Addressing Socioeconomic Disparities

Addressing socioeconomic disparities requires a multi-faceted approach that tackles their root causes and promotes inclusive economic growth and development. This includes implementing progressive tax policies, investing in education, healthcare, and social services, and strengthening labor rights and protections to ensure fair wages and working conditions for all workers.

Moreover, addressing systemic discrimination and marginalization is essential for reducing inequalities and promoting social justice. This includes implementing anti-discrimination laws and policies, promoting diversity and inclusion in education and employment, and addressing structural barriers to social mobility for marginalized groups.

Socioeconomic disparities represent a significant challenge to the stability, cohesion, and legitimacy of societies around the world. By perpetuating cycles of poverty, exclusion, and injustice, these disparities breed discord, undermining trust, solidarity, and cooperation within communities and fueling tensions and conflicts along lines of identity and ideology. However, by understanding the root causes of socioeconomic disparities and implementing policies to promote inclusive economic growth and social justice, we can work towards building a more equitable, resilient, and cohesive society where all individuals have the opportunity to thrive and contribute to the common good.

Cultural Clashes: Challenges to Global Harmony

Cultural clashes have emerged as significant obstacles to achieving global harmony in an increasingly interconnected world. As societies become more diverse and interconnected, differences in values, beliefs, and traditions often lead to tensions, misunderstandings, and conflicts. From clashes over religious beliefs and cultural practices to disputes over identity and heritage, cultural differences can fuel division, prejudice, and discrimination, hindering efforts to build inclusive and cohesive societies. In this chapter, we explore the nature of cultural clashes, their underlying causes, and their implications for global harmony and social cohesion.

The Nature of Cultural Clashes

Cultural clashes occur when individuals or groups with different cultural backgrounds come into contact and conflict with one another. These clashes can manifest in various forms, including religious conflicts, ethnic tensions, and clashes over social norms and values. They often arise from differences in worldview, belief systems, and practices that lead to misunderstandings, stereotypes, and prejudice.

At the heart of cultural clashes is the clash of identities and worldviews, where individuals and groups perceive their cultural practices and beliefs as superior or more legitimate than those of others. This can lead to feelings of superiority, ethnocentrism, and xenophobia, as well as a reluctance to engage with or accept alternative perspectives.

Causes of Cultural Clashes

Cultural clashes are driven by a variety of factors, including globalization, migration, and the erosion of traditional cultural boundaries. As societies become more interconnected through travel, trade, and technology, different cultures come into contact and competition with one another, leading to clashes over resources, territory, and influence.

Moreover, cultural clashes often arise from historical grievances, inequalities, and injustices that continue to shape the dynamics of contemporary society. Colonialism, imperialism, and globalization have imposed Western cultural norms and values on non-Western societies, leading to resistance, backlash, and cultural revitalization movements that seek to reclaim and preserve indigenous cultures and traditions.

Implications for Global Harmony

Cultural clashes have significant implications for global harmony, undermining efforts to build inclusive and cohesive societies that respect and celebrate diversity. When cultural differences are perceived as threats or sources of conflict, they can lead to social exclusion, discrimination, and violence, further deepening divisions and eroding trust and solidarity within communities.

Moreover, cultural clashes can exacerbate tensions between different religious, ethnic, and cultural groups, leading to intergroup conflicts and violence that destabilize regions and undermine peace and security. In an era of globalization and mass migration, managing cultural diversity and promoting intercultural dialogue and understanding are essential for fostering global harmony and peaceful coexistence.

Promoting Intercultural Dialogue and Understanding

Addressing cultural clashes requires a concerted effort to promote intercultural dialogue, understanding, and cooperation across diverse communities and societies. This includes initiatives to build bridges between different cultural and religious groups, promote empathy and tolerance, and challenge stereotypes and prejudices that fuel division and conflict.

Education plays a crucial role in fostering intercultural understanding and respect, teaching students about different cultures, religions, and worldviews, and promoting critical thinking and empathy. Moreover, cultural exchange programs, community dialogues, and grassroots initiatives can bring people from different backgrounds together to share their experiences, perspectives, and values, fostering empathy, mutual respect, and cooperation.

Cultural clashes represent significant challenges to achieving global harmony and social cohesion in an increasingly diverse and interconnected world. By understanding the nature of cultural clashes, their underlying causes, and their implications for social cohesion and peace, we can work towards building inclusive and cohesive societies that celebrate diversity and promote intercultural understanding and cooperation. Through dialogue, empathy, and mutual respect, we can bridge the divides that separate us and build a more peaceful, harmonious, and equitable world for future generations.

Chapter 4
The Human Element: Psychology of Conflict and Harmony

At the heart of every conflict and every instance of harmony lies the human element – the complex interplay of thoughts, emotions, and behaviors that shape our interactions with one another and the world around us. In this chapter, we delve into the psychology of conflict and harmony, exploring the underlying psychological processes that drive human behavior in times of discord and cooperation.

From the dynamics of prejudice and intergroup bias to the mechanisms of empathy and altruism, we examine the psychological factors that influence our perceptions, attitudes, and actions towards others. By understanding the psychological roots of conflict and harmony, we can gain insight into the mechanisms that drive human behavior and the strategies that can be employed to promote peace, understanding, and reconciliation.

Through the lens of psychology, we explore the complexities of human nature and the challenges of navigating the tumultuous waters of interpersonal and intergroup relations. By shedding light on the psychological underpinnings of conflict and harmony, we can foster greater empathy, compassion, and cooperation, paving the way towards a more peaceful and harmonious world.

Understanding Human Nature: Instincts and Tendencies

Human nature is a complex tapestry woven from the threads of biology, psychology, and culture. At its core lie a myriad of instincts and tendencies that have evolved over millennia to shape our behavior, thoughts, and emotions. In this exploration of human nature, we delve into the depths of our instincts and tendencies, seeking to unravel the mysteries of what drives us as individuals and as a species.

The Evolutionary Roots of Human Behavior

Much of human behavior can be traced back to our evolutionary past, shaped by the forces of natural selection and adaptation. Our ancestors faced myriad challenges in their quest for survival and reproduction, leading to the development of a range of adaptive behaviors and psychological mechanisms that helped them navigate their environment.

For example, the instinct for self-preservation drives us to seek food, shelter, and safety, while the drive for social connection motivates us to form bonds with others and seek out companionship and support. Similarly, the instinct for reproduction underlies our desire for sexual intimacy and the formation of romantic relationships, ensuring the continuation of the species.

The Influence of Psychology and Culture

While our evolutionary heritage provides a foundation for understanding human behavior, our actions are also influenced by psychological factors and cultural norms and values. Our minds are shaped by cognitive processes such as perception, memory, and decision-making, which filter and interpret the information we receive from the world around us.

Moreover, culture plays a powerful role in shaping our beliefs, attitudes, and behaviors, providing a framework of norms, values, and rituals that guide our interactions with others and the world. Cultural norms dictate everything from how we dress and speak to how we form relationships and express emotions, shaping our identity and sense of belonging within our social groups.

Instincts and Tendencies in Conflict and Harmony

Our instincts and tendencies can both drive conflict and foster harmony, depending on the context in which they are expressed. On the one hand, instincts such as fear, aggression, and tribalism can lead to conflicts between individuals and groups, as we compete for resources, status, and power.

On the other hand, instincts such as empathy, cooperation, and altruism can promote harmony and cooperation, as we work together to achieve common goals and support one another in times of need. These prosocial tendencies are deeply ingrained in human nature, reflecting our evolutionary heritage as social beings who rely on cooperation and mutual aid for survival and success.

Navigating the Tensions Between Conflict and Harmony

Navigating the tensions between conflict and harmony requires an understanding of the complex interplay between our instincts and tendencies and the social, cultural, and environmental factors that shape our behavior. While conflict may be inevitable at times, it is also possible to transcend our instinctual impulses and foster greater understanding, empathy, and cooperation.

One strategy for promoting harmony is through the cultivation of empathy and perspective-taking, which allows us to see the world through the eyes of others and understand their experiences and perspectives. By fostering empathy, we can bridge the divides that separate us and build connections based on shared humanity and understanding.

Additionally, promoting social cohesion and inclusivity can help mitigate the effects of conflict and promote a sense of belonging and unity within communities. By creating spaces for dialogue, collaboration, and mutual respect, we can foster environments where individuals and groups feel valued, respected, and supported, leading to greater harmony and cooperation.

Human nature is a complex mosaic of instincts and tendencies that shape our behavior, thoughts, and emotions. While conflicts may arise from our instinctual impulses, they are not inevitable, and it is possible to transcend our instincts and foster greater harmony and cooperation through empathy, understanding, and social cohesion. By understanding the roots of our behavior and promoting strategies for conflict resolution and reconciliation, we can work towards building a more peaceful and harmonious world for ourselves and future generations.

Cognitive Biases: Impediments to Harmony

Cognitive biases are inherent flaws in human reasoning and decision-making processes that can distort our perceptions, judgments, and actions. These biases, rooted in the way our brains process information, often lead us to make irrational or suboptimal choices, hindering our ability to understand others, resolve conflicts, and foster harmony. In this exploration of cognitive biases, we delve into their nature, mechanisms, and implications for social cohesion and harmony.

Understanding Cognitive Biases

Cognitive biases are mental shortcuts or heuristics that our brains use to process information quickly and efficiently. While these shortcuts can be useful in certain situations, they can also lead to systematic errors in judgment and decision-making when applied inappropriately.

One common type of cognitive bias is confirmation bias, where we tend to seek out and interpret information in a way that confirms our preexisting beliefs or hypotheses, while ignoring or discounting evidence that contradicts them. Similarly, availability bias leads us to overestimate the likelihood of events that are readily available in our memory, such as vivid or emotionally charged experiences, while underestimating the probability of less memorable events.

The Influence of Cognitive Biases on Social Relations

Cognitive biases play a significant role in shaping our perceptions and interactions with others, often leading to misunderstandings, conflicts, and divisions. For example, attribution bias causes us to attribute our own successes to internal factors such as skill or effort, while attributing our failures to external factors such as luck or circumstance. This can lead to feelings of superiority or inferiority in our interactions with others, undermining empathy and understanding.

Likewise, stereotype bias leads us to make assumptions about individuals based on their membership in a particular group, such as their race, gender, or nationality. These stereotypes can perpetuate prejudice and discrimination, leading to social tensions and inequalities that undermine trust and cooperation within communities.

Impediments to Harmony

Cognitive biases serve as significant impediments to harmony by distorting our perceptions, attitudes, and behaviors in ways that undermine empathy, understanding, and cooperation. When we are unaware of our biases or fail to recognize their influence, they can lead us to misinterpret the intentions and motivations of others, fueling mistrust, resentment, and conflict.

Moreover, cognitive biases can reinforce existing prejudices and stereotypes, leading to the perpetuation of social inequalities and injustices. For example, implicit bias—the unconscious associations we hold about certain groups—can lead to discriminatory behavior in hiring, education, and criminal justice, perpetuating systemic inequalities and hindering efforts to promote social cohesion and equality.

Mitigating the Impact of Cognitive Biases

While cognitive biases are pervasive and difficult to overcome, there are strategies we can employ to mitigate their impact and foster greater harmony and understanding. One approach is through awareness and education, helping individuals recognize and understand the nature of cognitive biases and their influence on behavior.

By cultivating mindfulness and self-reflection, we can become more attuned to our own biases and their effects on our perceptions and interactions with others. Additionally, promoting diversity and inclusion in our social networks and institutions can help challenge stereotypes and prejudices, fostering empathy and understanding across different groups.

Promoting Critical Thinking and Perspective-Taking

Encouraging critical thinking skills and perspective-taking can also help mitigate the impact of cognitive biases and promote harmony. By teaching individuals to question their assumptions, challenge their beliefs, and consider alternative viewpoints, we can foster a culture of openness, curiosity, and intellectual humility.

Moreover, promoting perspective-taking—the ability to see the world from the perspective of others—can help build empathy and understanding across diverse groups. By encouraging individuals to step outside of their own experiences and consider the experiences of others, we can bridge divides, build connections, and promote cooperation and harmony.

Cognitive biases are inherent flaws in human reasoning and decision-making processes that can hinder our ability to understand others, resolve conflicts, and foster harmony. By recognizing the nature of cognitive biases and their influence on behavior, we can work towards mitigating their impact and promoting greater empathy, understanding, and cooperation. Through awareness, education, and critical thinking, we can build a more inclusive and harmonious society where differences are respected, valued, and celebrated.

Empathy and Compassion: Building Blocks of Unity

Empathy and compassion are fundamental aspects of human nature that play a crucial role in fostering unity, understanding, and cooperation within societies. Rooted in our ability to understand and share the feelings of others, empathy allows us to connect with one another on a deep emotional level, while compassion motivates us to alleviate the suffering of others and act in ways that promote their well-being. In this exploration of empathy and compassion, we delve into their nature, mechanisms, and implications for social cohesion and unity.

Understanding Empathy

Empathy is the ability to understand and share the feelings, thoughts, and perspectives of others. It involves cognitive, emotional, and behavioral components, allowing us to mentally simulate the experiences of others and respond with appropriate emotions and actions. Empathy is a fundamental aspect of social cognition, enabling us to navigate complex social interactions, build relationships, and develop a sense of connection and belonging with others.

There are two main types of empathy: cognitive empathy, which involves understanding the thoughts and feelings of others from their perspective, and emotional empathy, which involves sharing and experiencing the emotions of others. Both types of empathy are essential for fostering understanding and connection with others, allowing us to recognize their needs, concerns, and experiences.

The Role of Compassion

Compassion is closely related to empathy but involves an additional component of action. While empathy involves understanding and sharing the feelings of others, compassion motivates us to alleviate their suffering and act in ways that promote their well-being. Compassion involves feelings of warmth, concern, and care for others, leading us to respond with kindness, generosity, and support.

Compassion is a powerful force for promoting unity and social cohesion, as it fosters a sense of shared humanity and interdependence. When we act with compassion towards others, we recognize their inherent worth and dignity as fellow human beings, transcending differences of race, religion, nationality, and culture.

Building Blocks of Unity

Empathy and compassion serve as the building blocks of unity, fostering connections and relationships that transcend individual differences and promote a sense of belonging and solidarity within communities. When we empathize with others and respond with compassion, we create spaces for understanding, support, and cooperation, strengthening social bonds and building resilient communities.

Empathy allows us to bridge divides and connect with others on a deep emotional level, fostering a sense of mutual understanding and respect. By putting ourselves in the shoes of others and seeing the world from their perspective, we can overcome differences and build bridges of empathy and understanding across diverse groups.

Compassion, meanwhile, motivates us to take action to alleviate the suffering of others and promote their well-being. Whether through acts of kindness, generosity, or support, compassion allows us to make a positive difference in the lives of others, fostering a culture of care and solidarity within communities.

Implications for Social Cohesion

Empathy and compassion have profound implications for social cohesion and unity, promoting a sense of belonging, trust, and cooperation within communities. When individuals feel understood, valued, and supported by others, they are more likely to contribute positively to the community and work towards common goals and objectives.

Moreover, empathy and compassion can help mitigate conflicts and tensions within communities, as individuals are more likely to resolve disputes peacefully and work towards reconciliation when they empathize with the perspectives and experiences of others. By fostering empathy and compassion, communities can build resilience in the face of adversity and create environments where everyone feels valued and respected.

Cultivating Empathy and Compassion

Cultivating empathy and compassion requires intentional effort and practice, as these qualities do not always come naturally to everyone. One strategy for cultivating empathy is through perspective-taking exercises, where individuals are encouraged to imagine themselves in the shoes of others and consider their thoughts, feelings, and experiences.

Similarly, cultivating compassion involves developing a mindset of kindness, generosity, and altruism towards others. This can be achieved through practices such as loving-kindness meditation, where individuals cultivate feelings of warmth, care, and compassion towards themselves and others.

Empathy and compassion are essential building blocks of unity, fostering connections and relationships that transcend individual differences and promote a sense of belonging and solidarity within communities. By understanding the nature of empathy and compassion and their implications for social cohesion, communities can work towards creating environments where everyone feels understood, valued, and supported. Through intentional effort and practice, we can cultivate empathy and compassion within ourselves and our communities, building a more inclusive, compassionate, and united society for all.

Chapter 5

Communication Breakdown: Barriers to Harmony

Communication is the lifeblood of human interaction, serving as the cornerstone of relationships, cooperation, and understanding within societies. However, despite its importance, communication is often fraught with challenges and barriers that hinder our ability to connect with others and foster harmony. In this chapter, we explore the various barriers to effective communication and their implications for social cohesion and unity.

From linguistic barriers and cultural differences to misinterpretations and misunderstandings, communication breakdowns can lead to conflicts, tensions, and divisions within communities. In an increasingly interconnected and diverse world, understanding and overcoming these barriers is essential for building inclusive and cohesive societies.

Through an exploration of the nature of communication breakdowns and their underlying causes, we seek to shed light on the challenges of effective communication and the strategies that can be employed to promote understanding, empathy, and cooperation. By addressing these barriers head-on, we can work towards creating environments where communication flourishes, connections deepen, and harmony prevails.

Miscommunication and Misunderstanding: Barriers to Harmony

Miscommunication and misunderstanding are pervasive challenges in human interaction, often leading to conflicts, tensions, and breakdowns in relationships. Despite our best intentions, communication can be fraught with errors and misinterpretations that hinder our ability to connect with others and foster harmony within societies. In this exploration of miscommunication and misunderstanding, we delve into their nature, mechanisms, and implications for social cohesion and unity.

Understanding Miscommunication

Miscommunication occurs when there is a discrepancy between the intended message of the sender and the interpreted message of the receiver. This discrepancy can arise from various factors, including linguistic differences, cultural norms, and cognitive biases that influence how information is encoded, transmitted, and decoded.

One common source of miscommunication is ambiguity in language, where words or phrases have multiple meanings or interpretations that can lead to confusion or misunderstanding. Additionally, nonverbal cues such as tone of voice, facial expressions, and body language can play a crucial role in communication but may be misinterpreted or overlooked, further complicating the exchange of information.

The Role of Assumptions and Expectations

Miscommunication is often exacerbated by assumptions and expectations that individuals bring to the communication process. We tend to interpret information based on our own beliefs, values, and experiences, leading us to make assumptions about others' intentions or motivations that may not align with reality.

Moreover, cultural differences in communication styles and norms can lead to misunderstandings, as individuals from different cultural backgrounds may have different expectations about how communication should occur. For example, cultures that value directness and assertiveness in communication may perceive indirect or nuanced messages as vague or unclear, leading to misinterpretations and conflicts.

Implications for Social Cohesion

Miscommunication and misunderstanding have significant implications for social cohesion and unity, as they can lead to breakdowns in relationships and trust within communities. When individuals feel misunderstood or misrepresented, they may become defensive or withdrawn, leading to further misunderstandings and conflicts.

Moreover, miscommunication can perpetuate stereotypes and prejudices, as individuals may rely on assumptions and generalizations to fill in gaps in their understanding of others. This can lead to the perpetuation of social inequalities and injustices, as marginalized groups may be unfairly judged or discriminated against based on misunderstandings or misinterpretations.

Strategies for Overcoming Miscommunication

Overcoming miscommunication and misunderstanding requires intentional effort and practice, as well as a willingness to listen, empathize, and communicate effectively with others. One strategy is active listening, where individuals strive to understand the perspectives and experiences of others without judgment or interruption.

Additionally, promoting cultural awareness and sensitivity can help reduce miscommunication by fostering understanding and respect for different communication styles and norms. By learning about the cultural backgrounds and values of others, individuals can adapt their communication strategies to better align with the expectations of diverse audiences.

Miscommunication and misunderstanding are pervasive challenges in human interaction that can hinder our ability to connect with others and foster harmony within societies. By understanding the nature of miscommunication and its underlying causes, communities can work towards creating environments where communication flourishes, connections deepen, and conflicts are resolved through dialogue and empathy. Through intentional effort and practice, we can overcome the barriers to effective communication and build inclusive and cohesive societies where everyone feels understood, valued, and respected.

Language and Cultural Differences: Navigating Diversity in Communication

Language and cultural differences are inherent aspects of human diversity that play a significant role in shaping how we communicate, interact, and understand one another. In an increasingly interconnected world, understanding and navigating these differences are essential for building inclusive and cohesive societies where communication flourishes and harmony prevails. In this exploration of language and cultural differences, we delve into their nature, mechanisms, and implications for social cohesion and unity.

The Diversity of Language

Language is a fundamental aspect of human communication, serving as a tool for expressing thoughts, emotions, and ideas. However, the diversity of languages spoken around the world reflects the richness and complexity of human culture and identity. From the thousands of languages spoken by indigenous peoples to the dialects and accents that vary within a single language, linguistic diversity is a testament to the uniqueness of human expression.

Language differences can pose significant challenges for communication, as individuals may struggle to understand one another due to differences in vocabulary, grammar, and syntax. Moreover, language barriers can hinder access to information, services, and opportunities, leading to social exclusion and inequality for speakers of minority or marginalized languages.

The Influence of Culture on Communication

Culture plays a crucial role in shaping how we communicate, as it encompasses the shared beliefs, values, norms, and practices of a particular group or society. Cultural differences in communication styles, norms, and expectations can lead to misunderstandings and conflicts, as individuals from different cultural backgrounds may interpret messages differently or have different expectations about how communication should occur.

For example, cultures vary in their preference for directness and indirectness in communication, with some cultures valuing explicit and straightforward communication, while others prefer more nuanced and indirect approaches. Additionally, cultural differences in nonverbal communication, such as gestures, facial expressions, and eye contact, can lead to misinterpretations and misunderstandings if not understood or acknowledged.

Implications for Social Cohesion

Language and cultural differences have profound implications for social cohesion and unity, as they can either enrich or hinder communication and understanding within communities. When individuals feel valued and respected for their linguistic and cultural identities, they are more likely to participate actively in society and contribute positively to the community.

Conversely, language and cultural barriers can lead to social exclusion and marginalization, as individuals may face discrimination or prejudice based on their linguistic or cultural background. This can contribute to feelings of alienation and disconnection, further exacerbating social divisions and tensions within communities.

Strategies for Navigating Language and Cultural Differences

Navigating language and cultural differences requires intentional effort and sensitivity, as well as a willingness to learn and adapt to the perspectives and experiences of others. One strategy is language learning and proficiency, which can help individuals bridge communication barriers and connect with speakers of different languages.

Additionally, promoting cultural awareness and sensitivity can help foster understanding and respect for different cultural norms and values. By learning about the customs, traditions, and beliefs of others, individuals can cultivate empathy and appreciation for diverse perspectives, reducing the likelihood of misunderstandings and conflicts.

Language and cultural differences are integral aspects of human diversity that shape how we communicate, interact, and understand one another. By understanding the nature of language and cultural differences and their implications for social cohesion, communities can work towards creating environments where communication flourishes, connections deepen, and harmony prevails. Through intentional effort and practice, we can navigate the complexities of linguistic and cultural diversity and build inclusive and cohesive societies where everyone feels valued, respected, and understood.

Digital Disconnect: Challenges in Online Communication

In today's digital age, communication has undergone a profound transformation, with the rise of the internet and social media platforms revolutionizing how we connect and interact with others. While these digital technologies offer unprecedented opportunities for communication and collaboration, they also present unique challenges that can hinder effective communication and understanding. In this exploration of the digital disconnect, we delve into the challenges of online communication and their implications for social cohesion and unity.

The Digital Landscape

The advent of the internet and social media has transformed communication, enabling instantaneous and global connectivity across diverse communities and cultures. However, the digital landscape is marked by a multitude of platforms, channels, and technologies that vary in their features, functions, and norms of interaction.

From email and messaging apps to social networking sites and virtual worlds, individuals have a plethora of tools at their disposal for communicating and sharing information online. While these platforms offer unprecedented access to information and opportunities for connection, they also present challenges related to privacy, security, and authenticity.

Challenges in Online Communication

Despite the benefits of digital communication, online interactions are often fraught with challenges that can hinder effective communication and understanding. One of the most significant challenges is the lack of nonverbal cues, such as tone of voice, facial expressions, and body language, which play a crucial role in conveying emotions and intentions in face-to-face communication.

Moreover, the asynchronous nature of many online interactions can lead to misinterpretations and misunderstandings, as individuals may not receive immediate feedback or clarification on their messages. This can be exacerbated by the brevity and ambiguity of digital communication, as messages may be misconstrued or taken out of context without the benefit of additional context or explanation.

The Influence of Digital Culture

Digital culture, characterized by rapid information exchange, viral trends, and online communities, also shapes how we communicate and interact online. The anonymity and distance afforded by digital platforms can lead to disinhibition and uncivil behavior, as individuals may feel emboldened to express opinions or engage in behaviors they would not in face-to-face interactions.

Moreover, the algorithmic nature of many online platforms can create echo chambers and filter bubbles, where individuals are exposed to information and perspectives that align with their existing beliefs and preferences. This can contribute to polarization and division within online communities, as individuals may be less exposed to diverse viewpoints and experiences.

Implications for Social Cohesion

The challenges of online communication have significant implications for social cohesion and unity, as they can hinder understanding, empathy, and connection within communities. When individuals feel misunderstood or misrepresented online, they may become defensive or withdrawn, leading to further misunderstandings and conflicts.

Moreover, the anonymity and distance of digital communication can contribute to a sense of detachment and disconnection from others, as individuals may not feel the same sense of accountability or responsibility for their actions online as they do in face-to-face interactions. This can undermine trust and cooperation within online communities, hindering efforts to build inclusive and cohesive societies.

Strategies for Navigating the Digital Disconnect

Navigating the digital disconnect requires intentional effort and strategies to promote empathy, understanding, and cooperation in online communication. One strategy is to promote digital literacy and critical thinking skills, helping individuals recognize and navigate the biases, algorithms, and pitfalls of online communication.

Additionally, fostering digital citizenship and online etiquette can help promote civility and respect in online interactions, creating environments where individuals feel safe and supported to express themselves authentically and respectfully. By promoting empathy, understanding, and connection in online communication, communities can work towards overcoming the challenges of the digital disconnect and building inclusive and cohesive digital spaces for all.

The digital disconnect presents unique challenges to effective communication and understanding in today's interconnected world. By understanding the nature of these challenges and their implications for social cohesion, communities can work towards creating digital environments where communication flourishes, connections deepen, and harmony prevails. Through intentional effort and strategies to promote empathy, understanding, and cooperation in online communication, we can navigate the complexities of the digital landscape and build inclusive and cohesive digital spaces for all.

Chapter 6
Bridging Divides: Strategies for Reconciliation

In a world marked by division, conflict, and polarization, the imperative to bridge divides and promote reconciliation has never been more urgent. Whether stemming from differences in ideology, culture, religion, or identity, divisions within societies can lead to mistrust, animosity, and violence, undermining social cohesion and unity. In this chapter, we explore strategies for reconciliation that seek to heal wounds, build bridges, and foster understanding and cooperation across divides.

Drawing on insights from conflict resolution, peacebuilding, and intergroup dialogue, we examine the principles and practices that can promote reconciliation and healing within communities. From truth and reconciliation processes to dialogue and mediation initiatives, we explore the diverse approaches that can facilitate meaningful engagement, empathy, and collaboration between conflicting parties.

Through an exploration of successful reconciliation efforts around the world, we highlight the importance of empathy, forgiveness, and mutual respect in overcoming divisions and building a more inclusive and harmonious society. By understanding the dynamics of conflict and reconciliation and embracing strategies that promote dialogue, understanding, and cooperation, communities can work towards healing past wounds and building a future where differences are respected, valued, and celebrated.

Dialogue and Mediation: Paths to Resolution

In societies marked by division and conflict, dialogue and mediation serve as essential pathways to resolution, offering constructive frameworks for addressing grievances, fostering understanding, and building bridges between conflicting parties. By providing spaces for open communication, empathy, and collaboration, dialogue and mediation facilitate the resolution of disputes and the promotion of reconciliation and peace. In this exploration of dialogue and mediation, we delve into their nature, mechanisms, and implications for conflict resolution and social cohesion.

Understanding Dialogue and Mediation

Dialogue is a process of open and respectful communication between individuals or groups with divergent perspectives or interests. It involves active listening, empathy, and a willingness to engage in constructive exchange, with the goal of building understanding and finding common ground.

Mediation, on the other hand, is a structured process facilitated by a neutral third party, known as a mediator, who helps conflicting parties communicate effectively, identify shared interests, and explore mutually acceptable solutions to their disputes. Mediation emphasizes collaboration, problem-solving, and compromise, empowering parties to reach agreements that address their needs and interests.

Principles of Effective Dialogue and Mediation

Effective dialogue and mediation are guided by principles of inclusivity, fairness, and empowerment, ensuring that all parties have the opportunity to participate fully and contribute to the resolution process. Key principles include:

1. **Neutrality and impartiality:** Mediators and facilitators must remain neutral and impartial, avoiding favoritism or bias towards any party involved in the conflict.

2. **Active listening:** Dialogue and mediation require participants to actively listen to one another's perspectives, experiences, and concerns, fostering empathy and understanding.

3. **Respect and dignity:** All participants in dialogue and mediation processes must be treated with respect and dignity, regardless of their backgrounds or viewpoints.

4. **Confidentiality:** Confidentiality is essential to create a safe and trusting environment for open communication, allowing parties to speak candidly without fear of reprisal or judgment.

Benefits of Dialogue and Mediation

Dialogue and mediation offer numerous benefits for conflict resolution and social cohesion. By providing structured frameworks for communication and problem-solving, they enable parties to address their grievances in a constructive and nonviolent manner, reducing the risk of escalation and further harm.

Moreover, dialogue and mediation promote understanding and empathy between conflicting parties, helping to humanize the "other" and break down stereotypes and prejudices. By fostering empathy and mutual respect, they lay the groundwork for reconciliation and cooperation, paving the way for sustainable peace and stability.

Applications of Dialogue and Mediation

Dialogue and mediation are applicable in a wide range of contexts, from interpersonal conflicts to large-scale societal disputes. They have been used successfully to resolve conflicts in areas such as family disputes, workplace disagreements, community tensions, and international conflicts.

For example, truth and reconciliation commissions have been established in countries such as South Africa and Rwanda to address historical injustices and promote healing and reconciliation in the aftermath of conflict and violence. These commissions provide opportunities for victims and perpetrators to share their experiences, acknowledge wrongdoing, and seek forgiveness, laying the foundation for reconciliation and peace.

Challenges and Considerations

While dialogue and mediation offer powerful tools for conflict resolution, they also face challenges and limitations. In some cases, deep-seated mistrust, power imbalances, and entrenched divisions may hinder meaningful dialogue and cooperation between conflicting parties.

Moreover, the effectiveness of dialogue and mediation depends on the willingness of parties to engage in good faith and abide by agreements reached through the process. Without genuine commitment to reconciliation and cooperation, dialogue and mediation efforts may fail to achieve lasting peace and stability.

Dialogue and mediation are indispensable tools for resolving conflicts, promoting understanding, and building bridges between conflicting parties. By providing structured frameworks for communication and problem-solving, they empower parties to address their grievances in a constructive and nonviolent manner, fostering empathy, reconciliation, and peace. Through their application in diverse contexts, dialogue and mediation offer pathways to resolution that honor the dignity and humanity of all involved, laying the groundwork for a more inclusive and harmonious society.

Building Trust and Understanding: Keys to Conflict Resolution and Social Cohesion

Trust and understanding are foundational elements of healthy relationships and cohesive societies. In contexts marked by division, conflict, and polarization, the cultivation of trust and understanding becomes essential for fostering reconciliation, cooperation, and peace. In this exploration of building trust and understanding, we delve into their nature, mechanisms, and implications for conflict resolution and social cohesion.

The Importance of Trust

Trust is the bedrock of any relationship, providing the foundation for cooperation, collaboration, and mutual support. In interpersonal relationships, trust is built through consistency, reliability, and integrity, as individuals demonstrate their commitment to honoring their promises and obligations.

Similarly, trust is essential for building effective institutions and systems of governance, as citizens rely on the trustworthiness of public officials and institutions to uphold the rule of law, protect human rights, and promote the common good. When trust is eroded, whether through corruption, abuse of power, or betrayal of trust, it can lead to widespread disillusionment, social unrest, and political instability.

The Role of Understanding

Understanding is closely intertwined with trust, as it involves the ability to empathize with others, recognize their perspectives and experiences, and communicate in ways that foster connection and mutual respect. In conflicts and disputes, understanding is essential for de-escalating tensions, bridging divides, and finding common ground.

Moreover, understanding requires active listening, empathy, and a willingness to engage with different viewpoints and experiences. By seeking to understand the motivations, fears, and aspirations of others, individuals can build empathy and compassion, fostering connections that transcend differences and promote reconciliation.

Strategies for Building Trust and Understanding

Building trust and understanding requires intentional effort and strategies that promote openness, transparency, and empathy. Key strategies include:

1. **Communication and Dialogue:** Open and honest communication is essential for building trust and understanding, as it provides opportunities for individuals to express their thoughts, feelings, and concerns in a safe and supportive environment. Dialogue processes, such as mediation and facilitated discussions, can help conflicting parties communicate effectively and explore mutually acceptable solutions to their disputes.

2. **Empathy and Perspective-Taking:** Empathy is the ability to understand and share the feelings of others, while perspective-taking involves stepping into the shoes of others and seeing the world from their perspective. By cultivating empathy and perspective-taking, individuals can build understanding and compassion for others, fostering connections that bridge divides and promote reconciliation.

3. **Transparency and Accountability:** Transparency and accountability are essential for building trust in institutions and systems of governance. When individuals and institutions are transparent about their actions, decisions, and intentions, they demonstrate their commitment to honesty, integrity, and fairness, fostering trust and confidence among stakeholders.

4. **Building Common Goals:** Finding common goals and objectives can help unite individuals and groups with diverse backgrounds and interests, fostering cooperation and collaboration towards shared objectives. By identifying common ground and working towards shared goals, conflicting parties can build trust and understanding, paving the way for reconciliation and peace.

Implications for Social Cohesion

Building trust and understanding has profound implications for social cohesion and unity, as it promotes resilience, cooperation, and mutual support within communities. When individuals trust one another and feel understood and valued, they are more likely to work together towards common goals and objectives, even in the face of challenges and adversity.

Moreover, trust and understanding foster a sense of belonging and inclusion within communities, as individuals feel respected and supported in expressing their identities, beliefs, and perspectives. By promoting an environment of trust and understanding, communities can create spaces where diversity is celebrated, conflicts are resolved peacefully, and everyone has the opportunity to thrive.

Challenges and Considerations

Building trust and understanding is not without its challenges, as it requires overcoming deep-seated mistrust, prejudice, and division within societies. In contexts marked by historical injustices, trauma, and conflict, building trust and understanding may require sustained effort, dialogue, and reconciliation processes that address the root causes of division and inequality.

Moreover, building trust and understanding requires commitment and participation from all stakeholders, as meaningful change cannot occur without the engagement and cooperation of those directly affected by conflict and injustice. Without genuine commitment to building trust and understanding, efforts to promote social cohesion and unity may fall short of their objectives.

Building trust and understanding are essential for promoting conflict resolution, social cohesion, and unity within societies. By fostering open communication, empathy, and cooperation, individuals and communities can bridge divides, resolve conflicts, and build resilient and inclusive societies where everyone feels valued and respected. Through intentional effort and strategies that promote trust and understanding, communities can create environments where differences are celebrated, conflicts are resolved peacefully, and everyone has the opportunity to thrive.

Conflict Transformation: Turning Discord into Opportunity

Conflict is an inevitable aspect of human interaction, arising from differences in beliefs, values, interests, and identities. While conflict is often viewed negatively, it also presents opportunities for growth, learning, and positive change. Conflict transformation is an approach that seeks to harness the constructive potential of conflict, turning discord into opportunities for reconciliation, understanding, and collaboration. In this exploration of conflict transformation, we delve into its principles, processes, and implications for building peace and fostering social cohesion.

Understanding Conflict Transformation

Conflict transformation differs from traditional approaches to conflict resolution in that it seeks to address the underlying causes and dynamics of conflict, rather than simply managing or resolving immediate disputes. It recognizes that conflict is a natural and inevitable part of human interaction, and that it can serve as a catalyst for positive change when approached constructively.

At its core, conflict transformation involves a shift in mindset from viewing conflict as inherently negative to seeing it as an opportunity for growth and transformation. It emphasizes the importance of empathy, dialogue, and collaboration in addressing the root causes of conflict and promoting reconciliation and peace.

Principles of Conflict Transformation

Conflict transformation is guided by several key principles that shape its approach to addressing conflict:

1. **Addressing Root Causes:** Conflict transformation seeks to address the underlying causes and drivers of conflict, rather than focusing solely on surface-level disputes. By addressing structural inequalities, injustices, and grievances, conflict transformation aims to create conditions for sustainable peace and social justice.

2. **Building Relationships:** Conflict transformation emphasizes the importance of building relationships and trust between conflicting parties. By fostering empathy, understanding, and respect, conflict transformation creates opportunities for dialogue and collaboration that can lead to reconciliation and mutual benefit.

3. **Promoting Inclusivity:** Conflict transformation promotes inclusivity and participation, ensuring that all stakeholders have a voice in the resolution process. By empowering marginalized and affected communities to participate in decision-making, conflict transformation fosters ownership and accountability for the outcomes of the process.

4. **Seeking Sustainable Solutions:** Conflict transformation seeks to find sustainable solutions to conflict that address the needs and interests of all parties involved. By promoting win-win outcomes and addressing the underlying drivers of conflict,

conflict transformation creates conditions for long-term peace and stability.

Processes of Conflict Transformation

Conflict transformation involves a series of processes and stages that unfold over time. These processes may include:

1. **Analysis and Assessment:** Conflict transformation begins with a thorough analysis and assessment of the root causes, dynamics, and stakeholders involved in the conflict. This stage involves gathering information, identifying key issues, and understanding the perspectives and interests of all parties.

2. **Dialogue and Engagement:** Dialogue and engagement are central to conflict transformation, providing opportunities for conflicting parties to communicate openly, express their concerns, and explore potential solutions. Facilitated dialogue processes, such as mediation and peacebuilding workshops, can help create spaces for constructive engagement and collaboration.

3. **Reconciliation and Healing:** Reconciliation and healing are important components of conflict transformation, as they address the emotional and psychological wounds caused by conflict. This may involve acknowledging past injustices, seeking forgiveness, and promoting healing through rituals, ceremonies, and community-based initiatives.

4. **Building Sustainable Peace:** Conflict transformation aims to build sustainable peace by addressing the root causes of conflict and promoting structural changes that address underlying inequalities and injustices. This may involve policy reforms, institutional changes, and efforts to promote social justice and human rights.

Implications for Social Cohesion

Conflict transformation has profound implications for social cohesion and unity, as it promotes a culture of dialogue, understanding, and collaboration that transcends differences and divisions. By addressing the root causes of conflict and promoting reconciliation and healing, conflict transformation creates conditions for communities to build trust, resilience, and solidarity.

Moreover, conflict transformation fosters a sense of ownership and agency among affected communities, empowering them to take an active role in shaping their own futures. By promoting inclusivity and participation, conflict transformation ensures that the voices of marginalized and affected groups are heard and respected, leading to more equitable and inclusive societies.

Challenges and Considerations

While conflict transformation offers a promising approach to addressing conflict, it also faces challenges and limitations. Deep-seated mistrust, power imbalances, and entrenched divisions may hinder efforts to promote dialogue and collaboration between conflicting parties. Moreover, conflict transformation requires sustained commitment and resources to address the underlying causes of conflict and promote reconciliation and peace.

Additionally, conflict transformation may encounter resistance from those who benefit from the status quo or who are unwilling to engage in dialogue and compromise. Overcoming these challenges requires creativity, persistence, and a willingness to challenge entrenched beliefs and attitudes that perpetuate conflict and division.

Conflict transformation offers a transformative approach to addressing conflict, turning discord into opportunities for reconciliation, understanding, and collaboration. By addressing the root causes of conflict and promoting dialogue, empathy, and inclusivity, conflict transformation creates conditions for sustainable peace and social cohesion. Through its emphasis on building relationships, seeking sustainable solutions, and promoting healing and reconciliation, conflict transformation empowers communities to build resilient and inclusive societies where everyone can thrive.

Chapter 7
Cultural Unity: Celebrating Diversity in Harmony

In a world characterized by diversity, cultural unity offers a vision of harmony that celebrates the richness and complexity of human expression. Cultural unity recognizes the value of diverse perspectives, traditions, and identities, seeking to foster mutual respect, understanding, and cooperation across cultural boundaries. Embracing diversity is fundamental to cultural unity, acknowledging that each culture contributes to the mosaic of human experience in its own unique way. Rather than seeking to homogenize or erase cultural differences, cultural unity celebrates the diversity of languages, beliefs, customs, and traditions that enrich our world. While cultural diversity is a source of strength, it can also present challenges to social cohesion and understanding. Cultural unity seeks to bridge divides and build connections between individuals and communities from different cultural backgrounds, finding common ground and shared values that transcend cultural differences. At its core, cultural unity promotes inclusivity and belonging, ensuring that all individuals and communities feel valued, respected, and empowered to contribute to society. By fostering an environment of mutual respect and appreciation for cultural diversity, cultural unity creates opportunities for dialogue, collaboration, and cooperation that strengthen social cohesion and build a more inclusive and harmonious world.

Cultural Exchange and Appreciation: Fostering Understanding and Connection

Cultural exchange and appreciation are integral to building bridges between diverse communities and fostering mutual understanding and respect. In an increasingly interconnected world, opportunities for cultural exchange abound, providing individuals and communities with the chance to learn from one another, celebrate diversity, and forge meaningful connections. In this exploration of cultural exchange and appreciation, we delve into their significance, mechanisms, and implications for promoting social cohesion and global citizenship.

The Significance of Cultural Exchange

Cultural exchange involves the sharing of ideas, traditions, customs, and perspectives between individuals and communities from different cultural backgrounds. It encompasses a wide range of activities, including language learning, artistic expression, culinary exploration, and intercultural dialogue. Cultural exchange fosters curiosity, openness, and empathy, as individuals immerse themselves in new experiences and engage with unfamiliar ways of life.

Moreover, cultural exchange promotes cross-cultural understanding and appreciation, challenging stereotypes and prejudices and fostering connections that transcend cultural boundaries. By learning about and engaging with diverse cultures, individuals gain a deeper appreciation for the complexities and richness of human experience, enriching their own lives and broadening their perspectives.

Mechanisms of Cultural Exchange

Cultural exchange takes place through various mechanisms and channels, ranging from formal educational programs to informal interactions and exchanges. Educational institutions, such as schools, universities, and cultural centers, play a crucial role in facilitating cultural exchange through study abroad programs, language courses, and intercultural workshops.

Additionally, technological advancements have expanded the reach and impact of cultural exchange, allowing individuals to connect with people from around the world through social media, online forums, and virtual platforms. These digital channels provide opportunities for cross-cultural dialogue and collaboration, transcending geographical barriers and fostering global connections.

Benefits of Cultural Exchange

Cultural exchange offers numerous benefits for individuals, communities, and societies as a whole. One of the primary benefits is the promotion of intercultural competence and communication skills, as individuals learn to navigate and interact with people from diverse cultural backgrounds. This enhances their ability to work collaboratively, solve problems creatively, and adapt to new and unfamiliar environments.

Moreover, cultural exchange fosters empathy, tolerance, and respect for diversity, as individuals develop a deeper understanding of the values, beliefs, and perspectives of others. By experiencing firsthand the richness and complexity of different cultures, individuals are better equipped to challenge stereotypes, combat prejudice, and promote social inclusion and equity.

Implications for Social Cohesion

Cultural exchange has significant implications for social cohesion and unity, as it promotes dialogue, understanding, and connection between individuals and communities from different cultural backgrounds. By fostering relationships built on mutual respect and appreciation, cultural exchange creates opportunities for collaboration and cooperation that transcend cultural divides.

Moreover, cultural exchange contributes to the creation of inclusive and harmonious societies, where diversity is celebrated as a source of strength and enrichment. By creating spaces for dialogue and engagement, cultural exchange empowers individuals to break down barriers, build bridges, and work towards common goals that benefit all members of society.

Challenges and Considerations

While cultural exchange offers numerous benefits, it also presents challenges and considerations that must be addressed to ensure its effectiveness and impact. One challenge is the risk of cultural appropriation, where aspects of marginalized or underrepresented cultures are appropriated and commodified without proper recognition or respect for their significance.

Additionally, cultural exchange must be approached with sensitivity and humility, recognizing the power dynamics and inequalities that exist between different cultures. It is essential to create opportunities for reciprocal exchange and mutual learning, where all parties involved have the opportunity to contribute and benefit from the exchange.

Cultural exchange and appreciation are essential components of building inclusive and cohesive societies that celebrate diversity and promote mutual understanding and respect. By facilitating dialogue, engagement, and collaboration between individuals and communities from different cultural backgrounds, cultural exchange creates opportunities for learning, growth, and connection that enrich our lives and strengthen our communities. Through intentional effort and commitment to fostering cross-cultural understanding and appreciation, we can create a more just, equitable, and harmonious world where everyone has the opportunity to thrive.

Cultural Competence: Navigating Differences Respectfully

In our increasingly interconnected world, cultural competence has emerged as a vital skill set for individuals and organizations seeking to navigate the complexities of diverse cultural landscapes. Cultural competence involves the ability to interact effectively and respectfully with people from different cultural backgrounds, recognizing and valuing the diversity of beliefs, customs, and perspectives that shape human experience. In this exploration of cultural competence, we delve into its importance, principles, and implications for promoting understanding and collaboration across cultures.

The Importance of Cultural Competence

Cultural competence is essential for building inclusive and harmonious societies where diversity is celebrated and respected. In today's globalized world, individuals and organizations interact with people from diverse cultural backgrounds on a daily basis, whether in the workplace, educational settings, or community spaces. Cultural competence enables individuals to navigate these interactions with sensitivity, empathy, and respect, fostering positive relationships and mutual understanding.

Moreover, cultural competence promotes social cohesion and unity by bridging divides and building connections between people from different cultural backgrounds. By fostering an environment of inclusivity and mutual respect, cultural competence creates opportunities for collaboration and cooperation that transcend cultural differences, leading to stronger and more resilient communities.

Principles of Cultural Competence

Cultural competence is guided by several key principles that shape its approach to interacting with people from diverse cultural backgrounds:

1. **Self-Awareness:** Cultural competence begins with self-awareness, as individuals reflect on their own cultural identity, biases, and assumptions. By examining their own beliefs and values, individuals can better understand how their cultural background influences their perceptions and interactions with others.

2. **Respect for Diversity:** Cultural competence involves respecting and valuing the diversity of beliefs, customs, and perspectives that exist within and across cultures. It requires an openness to learning from others and a willingness to embrace different ways of seeing the world.

3. **Empathy and Perspective-Taking:** Cultural competence requires empathy and perspective-taking, as individuals strive to understand the experiences and perspectives of people from different cultural backgrounds. By putting themselves in others' shoes, individuals can build connections and foster mutual understanding.

4. **Effective Communication:** Cultural competence involves effective communication skills that facilitate meaningful dialogue and interaction across cultural boundaries. This includes active listening, clear and respectful communication, and the ability to adapt one's communication style to accommodate cultural differences.

Implications for Social Cohesion

Cultural competence has significant implications for social cohesion and unity, as it promotes understanding, respect, and cooperation across cultural divides. By fostering relationships built on mutual respect and empathy, cultural competence creates opportunities for dialogue and collaboration that strengthen social bonds and build inclusive communities.

Moreover, cultural competence promotes equity and social justice by challenging stereotypes, prejudice, and discrimination based on cultural differences. By fostering environments where everyone feels valued and respected, cultural competence creates conditions for individuals and communities to thrive and contribute to society.

Applications of Cultural Competence

Cultural competence is applicable in a wide range of contexts, from interpersonal interactions to organizational and institutional settings. In the workplace, cultural competence enables employees to work effectively in diverse teams, collaborate with colleagues from different cultural backgrounds, and serve diverse customer bases.

In educational settings, cultural competence enhances learning outcomes by creating inclusive environments where students feel valued and respected for their cultural identities. By incorporating diverse perspectives and experiences into the curriculum, educators can enrich the learning experience and prepare students to thrive in an increasingly diverse world.

Challenges and Considerations

While cultural competence offers numerous benefits, it also presents challenges and considerations that must be addressed to ensure its effectiveness and impact. One challenge is the need for ongoing education and training to develop and maintain cultural competence skills. Cultural competence is a dynamic and evolving process that requires continuous learning and self-reflection to navigate the complexities of diverse cultural landscapes.

Additionally, cultural competence requires a commitment to addressing power imbalances and inequalities that perpetuate discrimination and exclusion based on cultural differences. It is essential to create environments where everyone has the opportunity to participate fully and contribute to decision-making processes, regardless of their cultural background.

Cultural competence is essential for building inclusive and harmonious societies where diversity is celebrated and respected. By fostering self-awareness, empathy, and effective communication skills, cultural competence enables individuals and organizations to navigate the complexities of diverse cultural landscapes with sensitivity and respect. Through intentional effort and commitment to promoting understanding and collaboration across cultures, we can create a more just, equitable, and inclusive world where everyone has the opportunity to thrive.

Fusion and Hybridization: Creating New Harmonies

Fusion and hybridization are dynamic processes through which diverse cultural elements blend and interact, giving rise to innovative forms of expression, identity, and creativity. In an increasingly interconnected world, cultural fusion and hybridization have become prevalent phenomena, shaping the way we perceive and engage with culture. In this exploration of fusion and hybridization, we delve into their significance, mechanisms, and implications for fostering creativity, diversity, and social cohesion.

Understanding Fusion and Hybridization

Fusion refers to the blending or merging of distinct cultural elements to create something new and unique. It involves the synthesis of diverse influences, traditions, and styles, often resulting in hybrid forms that defy categorization and challenge traditional notions of cultural identity. Hybridization, on the other hand, refers to the process through which cultural elements from different traditions or backgrounds come into contact and interact, leading to the emergence of hybrid cultural practices, artifacts, and identities.

Fusion and hybridization can occur in various domains, including music, art, literature, cuisine, fashion, and language. They are often driven by factors such as globalization, migration, colonization, and technological advancements, which facilitate cross-cultural exchange and interaction on a global scale.

Mechanisms of Fusion and Hybridization

Fusion and hybridization occur through a variety of mechanisms and processes that facilitate the mixing and blending of cultural elements. These mechanisms may include:

1. **Cross-Cultural Exchange:** Cross-cultural exchange involves the sharing and diffusion of cultural practices, beliefs, and artifacts between different cultural groups. It can occur through migration, trade, colonization, tourism, media, and technology, creating opportunities for cultural elements to come into contact and interact.

2. **Cultural Appropriation:** Cultural appropriation refers to the borrowing or adoption of elements from one culture by members of another culture, often without proper acknowledgment or respect for their significance. While cultural appropriation can perpetuate harmful stereotypes and power imbalances, it can also contribute to cultural fusion and hybridization when done respectfully and collaboratively.

3. **Cultural Syncretism:** Cultural syncretism involves the blending or reconciliation of different cultural beliefs, practices, and traditions to create new syncretic forms. It often occurs in contexts where cultures come into contact and interact, leading to the emergence of hybrid religious, spiritual, and artistic expressions.

4. **Globalization:** Globalization has facilitated the spread and exchange of cultural practices and influences on a global scale,

leading to increased cultural fusion and hybridization. Advances in communication, transportation, and technology have made it easier for people to connect and interact across geographical and cultural boundaries, resulting in the emergence of new cultural forms and identities.

Implications of Fusion and Hybridization

Fusion and hybridization have profound implications for creativity, diversity, and social cohesion. By bringing together diverse cultural elements, they foster innovation and creativity, giving rise to new artistic, musical, and literary forms that challenge conventions and push boundaries. Cultural fusion and hybridization also contribute to cultural diversity and pluralism, enriching our understanding of the complexity and richness of human experience.

Moreover, fusion and hybridization promote social cohesion and unity by fostering connections and shared experiences across cultural divides. They create opportunities for dialogue, collaboration, and mutual understanding, as people come together to celebrate and explore their commonalities and differences. By embracing cultural fusion and hybridization, societies can build inclusive and harmonious communities where diversity is celebrated as a source of strength and resilience.

Examples of Fusion and Hybridization

Fusion and hybridization can be observed in a wide range of cultural expressions and practices around the world. In music, genres such as jazz, reggae, hip-hop, and salsa have emerged through the fusion of different musical traditions and styles. Similarly, in cuisine, fusion cuisine blends ingredients and cooking techniques from different culinary traditions to create innovative and eclectic dishes.

In fashion, designers often draw inspiration from diverse cultural sources, combining elements from different traditions and eras to create unique and hybridized styles. In literature and art, artists and writers explore themes of cultural identity, migration, and globalization, creating works that reflect the complexities and nuances of contemporary cultural landscapes.

Challenges and Considerations

While fusion and hybridization offer opportunities for creativity and cultural exchange, they also present challenges and considerations that must be addressed. One challenge is the risk of cultural commodification and exploitation, where cultural elements are appropriated and commercialized for profit without proper acknowledgment or respect for their significance.

Additionally, fusion and hybridization can raise questions of authenticity and cultural ownership, particularly when cultural elements are taken out of their original context or appropriated by dominant cultural groups. It is essential to approach fusion and hybridization with sensitivity and respect for the cultural integrity and autonomy of the communities involved.

Fusion and hybridization are dynamic processes through which diverse cultural elements blend and interact, giving rise to new forms of expression, identity, and creativity. They foster innovation, diversity, and social cohesion by bringing together people from different cultural backgrounds to celebrate and explore their commonalities and differences. By embracing fusion and hybridization, societies can build inclusive and harmonious communities where diversity is celebrated as a source of strength and resilience, paving the way for a more interconnected and harmonious world.

Chapter 8
Political Unity: Building Consensus in a Polarized World

In an era marked by deep political divisions and ideological polarization, the pursuit of political unity has become an increasingly urgent imperative. Political unity involves the forging of consensus and cooperation among diverse stakeholders to address common challenges and advance shared goals. However, in a world characterized by competing interests, entrenched ideologies, and social fragmentation, building political unity presents formidable challenges. The need for political unity is paramount in addressing complex issues like climate change, economic inequality, public health crises, and geopolitical conflicts. Partisan gridlock and ideological polarization can hinder progress and undermine public trust in democratic institutions, making political unity crucial for mobilizing collective resources and expertise to tackle shared problems.

Challenges to Political Unity:

Achieving political unity requires overcoming a range of obstacles, including deep-seated ideological divisions, partisan polarization, and distrust in political institutions. In an increasingly interconnected and diverse world, competing interests and values can make consensus-building a daunting task. Moreover, the rise of populist movements, disinformation campaigns, and social media echo chambers has further exacerbated political polarization, making it difficult to bridge the gap between opposing viewpoints.

Strategies for Building Political Unity:

Building political unity requires intentional effort and a commitment to dialogue, compromise, and inclusive decision-making processes. Key strategies may include fostering cross-party collaboration, promoting civic engagement and participation, and investing in inclusive governance structures that prioritize transparency, accountability, and responsiveness to the needs of all citizens. Additionally, promoting a culture of empathy, respect, and civility in political discourse can help reduce animosity and bridge divides between opposing factions.

Implications for Social Cohesion:

Political unity has profound implications for social cohesion and democratic governance, as it fosters trust, cooperation, and solidarity among citizens and between different levels of government. By transcending partisan divides and promoting inclusive decision-making processes, political unity creates opportunities for citizens to engage meaningfully in the democratic process and contribute to the common good. Moreover, political unity promotes stability and resilience in the face of external threats and challenges, strengthening the social fabric and fostering a sense of collective belonging and identity.

Political unity is essential for addressing the complex and interconnected challenges facing societies today. By fostering consensus, cooperation, and inclusive decision-making processes, political unity offers a pathway towards effective governance, social cohesion, and democratic participation. While achieving political unity may be challenging in a polarized world, it is essential for building resilient and inclusive societies where all citizens have the opportunity to thrive and contribute to the common good.

Finding Common Ground: Principles of Consensus Building

In today's increasingly polarized and divisive political landscape, the ability to find common ground and build consensus is more important than ever. Consensus building involves bringing together diverse stakeholders to identify shared interests, goals, and values, and to develop mutually acceptable solutions to complex problems. It requires effective communication, negotiation, and collaboration to bridge divides and create space for constructive dialogue and compromise. In this exploration of consensus building, we delve into its principles, strategies, and implications for fostering effective governance, social cohesion, and democratic participation.

Understanding Consensus Building

Consensus building is a collaborative process through which stakeholders work together to reach agreement on contentious issues or decisions. Unlike traditional decision-making processes that rely on majority rule or hierarchical authority, consensus building emphasizes the importance of inclusivity, participation, and mutual respect. It seeks to find win-win solutions that address the needs and concerns of all parties involved, rather than imposing decisions unilaterally or perpetuating power imbalances.

Principles of Consensus Building

Consensus building is guided by several key principles that shape its approach to resolving conflicts and reaching agreements:

1. **Inclusivity:** Consensus building requires the active participation of all stakeholders affected by the decision or issue at hand. It involves creating opportunities for diverse voices to be heard and valued, ensuring that everyone has a seat at the table and an opportunity to contribute to the decision-making process.

2. **Transparency:** Consensus building relies on transparency and openness in communication and decision-making. It involves sharing information openly, honestly, and in a timely manner, so that all stakeholders have access to relevant information and can make informed decisions.

3. **Mutual Respect:** Consensus building fosters an environment of mutual respect and civility, where all parties treat each other with dignity and consideration. It involves acknowledging and valuing the perspectives, experiences, and interests of others, even when they differ from one's own.

4. **Flexibility:** Consensus building requires flexibility and adaptability in approach, as stakeholders navigate complex and evolving dynamics. It involves being open to new ideas, perspectives, and solutions, and being willing to adjust course in response to changing circumstances or feedback.

5. **Commitment to Action:** Consensus building is not just about reaching agreement; it also involves a commitment to implementing agreed-upon solutions and following through on collective decisions. It requires accountability and responsibility from all parties involved, as they work together to turn consensus into action.

Strategies for Consensus Building

Consensus building involves a variety of strategies and techniques for facilitating dialogue, negotiation, and collaboration among stakeholders. Some key strategies include:

1. **Active Listening:** Consensus building begins with active listening, as stakeholders seek to understand each other's perspectives, interests, and concerns. It involves listening with empathy and openness, without judgment or interruption, and seeking clarification when needed.

2. **Identifying Common Ground:** Consensus building focuses on identifying areas of common ground and shared interests among stakeholders. It involves finding points of agreement and building on them to develop mutually acceptable solutions that meet the needs of all parties involved.

3. **Exploring Creative Solutions:** Consensus building encourages creativity and innovation in problem-solving, as stakeholders brainstorm and explore a wide range of possible solutions. It involves thinking outside the box and considering unconventional approaches that may address underlying issues more effectively.

4. **Facilitated Dialogue:** Consensus building often involves facilitated dialogue processes, where trained facilitators guide stakeholders through structured conversations and decision-making processes. Facilitators help create a safe and inclusive space for dialogue, ensure that all voices are heard, and facilitate productive exchanges of ideas and perspectives.

5. **Negotiation and Compromise:** Consensus building requires negotiation and compromise to bridge differences and reach agreement. It involves finding mutually acceptable trade-offs and concessions that balance competing interests and priorities, while still advancing shared goals and values.

Implications for Effective Governance

Consensus building has significant implications for effective governance, as it promotes collaboration, cooperation, and trust among stakeholders. By involving diverse voices in decision-making processes and prioritizing inclusivity and transparency, consensus building enhances the legitimacy and effectiveness of government policies and programs. Moreover, consensus building fosters a sense of ownership and accountability among stakeholders, as they work together to develop solutions that address shared challenges and priorities.

Implications for Social Cohesion

Consensus building also has implications for social cohesion and community resilience, as it fosters dialogue, understanding, and cooperation among diverse stakeholders. By creating opportunities for constructive engagement and collaboration, consensus building builds bridges across divides and strengthens social bonds and trust. Moreover, consensus building promotes a sense of collective ownership and responsibility for addressing common challenges, fostering a shared sense of identity and belonging among members of the community.

Consensus building is essential for addressing complex challenges and promoting effective governance, social cohesion, and democratic participation. By fostering inclusivity, transparency, and mutual respect, consensus building creates opportunities for stakeholders to come together, find common ground, and develop solutions that benefit all members of society. While consensus building may be challenging and time-consuming, its long-term benefits in terms of building trust, cooperation, and resilience make it a valuable approach for navigating the complexities of our increasingly interconnected and diverse world.

Political Reconciliation: Healing Divisions

Political reconciliation is a process of healing and rebuilding trust in the aftermath of conflict, division, or oppression. It involves acknowledging past injustices, addressing grievances, and fostering dialogue and cooperation among former adversaries to build a more inclusive and harmonious society. In this exploration of political reconciliation, we delve into its principles, strategies, and implications for fostering healing, justice, and social cohesion in divided societies.

Understanding Political Reconciliation

Political reconciliation is grounded in the recognition of past wrongs and the commitment to moving forward together towards a shared future. It goes beyond mere forgiveness or forgetting, seeking to address the root causes of conflict and division and to create conditions for lasting peace and stability. Political reconciliation is often associated with transitions from authoritarianism to democracy, post-conflict peacebuilding efforts, and efforts to address historical injustices such as apartheid, colonialism, or genocide.

Principles of Political Reconciliation

Political reconciliation is guided by several key principles that shape its approach to healing divisions and rebuilding trust:

1. **Truth and Reconciliation:** Political reconciliation involves confronting the truth about past injustices and human rights abuses, and acknowledging the suffering of victims and survivors. Truth and reconciliation commissions, such as those established in South Africa and Rwanda, provide forums for victims to share their experiences and for perpetrators to take responsibility for their actions.

2. **Justice and Accountability:** Political reconciliation requires accountability for past crimes and violations of human rights. This may involve prosecuting perpetrators of violence and injustice, providing reparations to victims, and reforming institutions to prevent future abuses. Justice is essential for addressing grievances and restoring the rule of law, and for building trust in the reconciliation process.

3. **Inclusivity and Participation:** Political reconciliation involves the active participation of all stakeholders affected by conflict or division. It requires creating opportunities for dialogue and collaboration among former adversaries, as well as engaging

with marginalized and excluded groups to ensure that their voices are heard and their needs are addressed.

4. **Forgiveness and Healing:** Political reconciliation requires a commitment to forgiveness and healing, both for individuals and for society as a whole. Forgiveness does not mean forgetting or excusing past wrongs, but rather acknowledging the humanity of both victims and perpetrators and seeking to break the cycle of revenge and retribution.

Strategies for Political Reconciliation

Political reconciliation involves a variety of strategies and approaches for fostering healing, justice, and social cohesion:

1. **Dialogue and Mediation:** Political reconciliation often begins with dialogue and mediation efforts aimed at bringing together former adversaries to discuss their grievances and aspirations. Facilitated dialogue processes provide opportunities for frank and open discussions, as well as for building trust and understanding between conflicting parties.

2. **Transitional Justice:** Transitional justice mechanisms, such as truth commissions, tribunals, and reparations programs, play a crucial role in addressing past injustices and providing redress for victims. These mechanisms help to uncover the truth about past abuses, hold perpetrators accountable, and provide reparations to victims, while also promoting reconciliation and healing.

3. **Community Reintegration:** Political reconciliation involves efforts to reintegrate former combatants and marginalized groups into society, and to address the root causes of conflict, such as poverty, inequality, and discrimination. This may involve providing job training, education, and economic

opportunities to former combatants, as well as promoting social inclusion and reconciliation at the community level.

4. **Education and Awareness:** Political reconciliation requires educating the public about the causes and consequences of conflict, and about the importance of reconciliation and social cohesion. This may involve curriculum reform to include lessons on human rights, peacebuilding, and conflict resolution in schools, as well as public awareness campaigns and commemorative events to acknowledge past injustices and promote reconciliation.

Implications for Healing Divisions

Political reconciliation has profound implications for healing divisions and rebuilding trust in divided societies. By addressing past injustices, promoting accountability, and fostering dialogue and cooperation among former adversaries, political reconciliation creates opportunities for healing, forgiveness, and social cohesion. It helps to break down barriers of mistrust and resentment, and to build bridges of understanding and solidarity between conflicting groups. Moreover, political reconciliation contributes to building a more resilient and inclusive society, where all members feel valued, respected, and empowered to contribute to the common good.

Political reconciliation is a complex and challenging process that requires commitment, courage, and perseverance. By addressing past injustices, promoting accountability, and fostering dialogue and cooperation among former adversaries, political reconciliation offers a pathway towards healing divisions and building a more inclusive and harmonious society. While the road to reconciliation may be long and difficult, its benefits in terms of fostering healing, justice, and social cohesion make it a crucial endeavor for societies emerging from conflict, division, or oppression. Through sustained effort and a commitment to building bridges of understanding and cooperation, political reconciliation offers hope for a brighter and more peaceful future for all.

Strengthening Democratic Institutions: Promoting Accountability, Participation, and Resilience

Democratic institutions form the backbone of any democratic society, providing the framework for governance, representation, and the protection of fundamental rights and freedoms. However, in recent years, democratic institutions have faced numerous challenges, including erosion of trust, polarization, and threats to the rule of law. Strengthening democratic institutions is essential for safeguarding democracy and promoting good governance, accountability, and social cohesion. In this exploration of strengthening democratic institutions, we delve into its importance, strategies, and implications for fostering a vibrant and resilient democracy.

The Importance of Democratic Institutions

Democratic institutions play a crucial role in ensuring that power is exercised responsibly, transparently, and in the public interest. They provide mechanisms for citizens to participate in decision-making processes, hold elected officials accountable, and protect individual rights and freedoms. Strong democratic institutions are essential for promoting political stability, social cohesion, and economic prosperity, as well as for preventing abuses of power and corruption.

Challenges Facing Democratic Institutions

Despite their importance, democratic institutions face numerous challenges that threaten their effectiveness and legitimacy. These challenges may include:

1. **Erosion of Trust:** Declining trust in democratic institutions, such as governments, parliaments, and political parties,

undermines their ability to govern effectively and represent the interests of all citizens.

2. **Polarization:** Increasing polarization and divisiveness within society can hinder cooperation and compromise within democratic institutions, leading to gridlock and paralysis.

3. **Corruption and Abuse of Power:** Corruption and the abuse of power undermine the integrity and credibility of democratic institutions, eroding public confidence and trust in the democratic process.

4. **Threats to the Rule of Law:** Attacks on the rule of law, including attempts to undermine judicial independence and weaken checks and balances, pose a significant threat to democratic institutions and principles.

Strategies for Strengthening Democratic Institutions

Strengthening democratic institutions requires a comprehensive approach that addresses both institutional weaknesses and broader societal challenges. Some key strategies may include:

1. **Promoting Transparency and Accountability:** Enhancing transparency and accountability mechanisms within democratic institutions is essential for preventing corruption and abuse of power. This may involve measures such as strengthening oversight bodies, increasing public access to information, and promoting financial transparency and disclosure.

2. **Fostering Civic Engagement and Participation:** Increasing citizen engagement and participation in the democratic process is essential for ensuring that democratic institutions are responsive to the needs and aspirations of all citizens. This may involve measures such as expanding access to voting, promoting civil society activism, and encouraging citizen participation in decision-making processes.

3. **Protecting Human Rights and the Rule of Law:** Upholding human rights and the rule of law is fundamental to the integrity and credibility of democratic institutions. This may involve measures such as strengthening judicial independence, protecting freedom of expression and assembly, and ensuring equal protection under the law for all citizens.

4. **Building Institutional Capacity:** Strengthening the capacity of democratic institutions to perform their functions effectively is essential for promoting good governance and accountability. This may involve measures such as providing training and professional development for public officials, investing in infrastructure and technology, and streamlining bureaucratic processes.

Implications of Strengthening Democratic Institutions

Strengthening democratic institutions has profound implications for democracy, governance, and social cohesion:

1. **Promoting Political Stability:** Strong democratic institutions contribute to political stability by providing mechanisms for peaceful resolution of conflicts and disputes, and by ensuring that power is transferred peacefully through free and fair elections.

2. **Enhancing Legitimacy and Trust:** Strengthening democratic institutions enhances their legitimacy and trustworthiness in the eyes of the public, fostering confidence in the democratic process and promoting social cohesion.

3. Fostering Inclusive Development: Strong democratic institutions create an enabling environment for inclusive and sustainable development, by promoting transparency, accountability, and participation in decision-making processes.

4. **Protecting Human Rights:** Strengthening democratic institutions helps protect human rights and fundamental freedoms, by providing mechanisms for redress and accountability in cases of abuse or violation.

Strengthening democratic institutions is essential for safeguarding democracy and promoting good governance, accountability, and social cohesion. By addressing challenges such as erosion of trust, polarization, and threats to the rule of law, democratic institutions can better fulfill their roles in representing the interests of all citizens, protecting human rights, and promoting inclusive development. Through a combination of transparency, accountability, civic engagement, and respect for the rule of law, democratic institutions can build resilience and adaptability in the face of evolving challenges, ensuring that democracy remains a vibrant and enduring form of governance.

Chapter 9

Economic Harmony: Addressing Disparities and Inequality

Economic harmony is not merely about achieving high GDP growth or maximizing profit margins; rather, it encompasses the equitable distribution of wealth, opportunities, and resources to ensure the well-being and prosperity of all members of society. In this chapter, we explore the concept of economic harmony and its significance in addressing disparities and inequality. While economic growth is essential for development, it must be accompanied by policies and strategies that promote inclusive growth, reduce poverty, and narrow the gap between the rich and the poor. By addressing disparities and inequality, economic harmony fosters social cohesion, promotes sustainable development, and builds a more resilient and inclusive economy. In this exploration of economic harmony, we delve into its principles, challenges, and implications for fostering prosperity and well-being for all members of society.

Wealth Redistribution: Tackling Economic Disparities

Wealth redistribution is a fundamental component of efforts to address economic disparities and promote greater equity within society. Economic inequality, characterized by significant disparities in income and wealth distribution, undermines social cohesion, stifles economic growth, and undermines democratic principles. Wealth redistribution seeks to rectify these imbalances by implementing policies and mechanisms that reallocate resources from the wealthy to the less affluent, thereby promoting a more equitable distribution of wealth and opportunities. In this exploration of wealth redistribution, we delve into its principles, strategies, challenges, and implications for fostering economic justice and social cohesion.

Understanding Wealth Redistribution

Wealth redistribution is based on the principle of social justice, which holds that resources and opportunities should be distributed fairly and equitably among all members of society. It recognizes that unbridled capitalism and market forces alone often lead to widening economic disparities and perpetuate cycles of poverty and privilege. Wealth redistribution aims to counteract these tendencies by implementing policies and programs that transfer resources from those who have accumulated wealth and privilege to those who are less fortunate, thereby leveling the playing field and providing a more equal opportunity for all.

Strategies for Wealth Redistribution

Wealth redistribution can take various forms, including:

1. **Progressive Taxation:** Progressive taxation involves levying higher tax rates on individuals or households with higher incomes or greater wealth. This approach ensures that those who can afford to contribute more to society do so, while providing essential services and support to those in need. Progressive taxation can include income taxes, capital gains taxes, inheritance taxes, and other forms of wealth taxation.

2. **Social Welfare Programs:** Social welfare programs provide direct assistance and support to individuals and families facing financial hardship or disadvantage. These programs may include unemployment benefits, social security, food assistance, housing subsidies, and healthcare coverage. By providing a safety net for those in need, social welfare programs help to

mitigate the impact of economic inequality and promote social inclusion and well-being.

3. **Minimum Wage Laws:** Minimum wage laws establish a floor on wages, ensuring that workers are paid a decent and livable wage for their labor. By setting a minimum standard for wages, minimum wage laws help to reduce poverty and inequality, while also stimulating consumer demand and economic growth.

4. **Wealth and Asset Redistribution:** Wealth and asset redistribution policies aim to address the concentration of wealth and power in the hands of a few by promoting greater ownership and control of assets among the broader population. This may involve measures such as land reform, asset redistribution programs, and policies to promote employee ownership and cooperative enterprises.

Challenges and Considerations

Wealth redistribution faces several challenges and considerations, including:

1. **Political Resistance:** Wealth redistribution often faces political resistance from powerful vested interests who stand to lose from more equitable distribution of resources. Lobbying efforts, campaign contributions, and ideological opposition can hinder efforts to implement progressive taxation and social welfare programs.

2. **Economic Efficiency:** Critics argue that wealth redistribution may reduce economic incentives and disincentivize entrepreneurship and investment, thereby stifling economic growth and innovation. Finding the right balance between equity and efficiency is essential to ensure that wealth redistribution policies promote both social justice and economic prosperity.

3. **Administrative Complexity:** Wealth redistribution programs can be administratively complex and costly to implement, requiring robust systems for taxation, social assistance, and wealth management. Ensuring transparency, accountability, and efficiency in the administration of wealth redistribution programs is essential to their success.

4. **Social Cohesion:** Wealth redistribution can have implications for social cohesion and solidarity, as it may be perceived as unfairly benefiting certain groups at the expense of others. Building public support and consensus for wealth redistribution policies requires fostering a sense of shared responsibility and mutual obligation among all members of society.

Implications for Economic Justice and Social Cohesion

Wealth redistribution has profound implications for economic justice and social cohesion. By promoting a more equitable distribution of wealth and opportunities, wealth redistribution policies help to reduce poverty, narrow economic disparities, and build a more inclusive and resilient economy. Moreover, wealth redistribution fosters social cohesion by reducing social exclusion and marginalization, promoting social mobility and upward economic mobility, and fostering a sense of solidarity and shared purpose among all members of society.

Wealth redistribution is a critical tool for addressing economic disparities and promoting greater equity and social justice within society. By implementing progressive taxation, social welfare programs, minimum wage laws, and wealth redistribution policies, societies can ensure that resources and opportunities are distributed more fairly and equitably among all members of society. While wealth redistribution may face challenges and resistance, its benefits in terms of promoting economic justice, social cohesion, and shared prosperity make it a crucial component of efforts to build a more just and inclusive society. Through sustained efforts and a commitment to social justice and solidarity, wealth redistribution can help to create a more equitable and sustainable future for all.

Inclusive Growth: Fostering Opportunities for All

Inclusive growth is a development strategy that seeks to ensure that the benefits of economic growth are shared equitably among all segments of society, particularly those who are marginalized or disadvantaged. Unlike traditional approaches to economic development, which focus solely on increasing GDP or per capita income, inclusive growth emphasizes the importance of creating opportunities for all individuals to participate in and benefit from the growth process. In this exploration of inclusive growth, we delve into its principles, strategies, challenges, and implications for fostering social justice, economic prosperity, and sustainable development.

Understanding Inclusive Growth

Inclusive growth is rooted in the recognition that economic growth alone is insufficient for reducing poverty and inequality, and that it must be accompanied by policies and strategies that promote social inclusion, equality of opportunity, and human development. Inclusive growth prioritizes investments in education, healthcare, infrastructure, and social protection, as well as measures to promote decent work, gender equality, and environmental sustainability. By ensuring that the benefits of growth reach all members of society, inclusive growth helps to build a more resilient, equitable, and prosperous economy.

Principles of Inclusive Growth

Inclusive growth is guided by several key principles that shape its approach to promoting equitable and sustainable development:

1. **Equity and Social Justice:** Inclusive growth prioritizes the needs and interests of the most vulnerable and marginalized members of society, including women, children, ethnic minorities, persons with disabilities, and indigenous communities. It seeks to reduce disparities in income, wealth, and opportunities, and to address the root causes of poverty and exclusion.

2. **Equality of Opportunity:** Inclusive growth emphasizes the importance of creating opportunities for all individuals to participate in and benefit from the growth process, regardless of their background or circumstances. This may involve measures to promote access to education, healthcare, employment, and financial services, as well as efforts to eliminate discrimination and barriers to social mobility.

3. **Sustainability and Resilience:** Inclusive growth recognizes the interdependence of social, economic, and environmental factors, and seeks to promote development that is sustainable and resilient over the long term. This may involve investments in renewable energy, climate adaptation, sustainable agriculture, and ecosystem conservation, as well as measures to promote green technology and innovation.

4. **Partnership and Participation:** Inclusive growth involves collaboration and partnership among government, civil society, the private sector, and other stakeholders to design and implement policies and programs that promote social inclusion and economic opportunity. It also emphasizes the importance of meaningful participation and consultation with affected communities in decision-making processes.

Strategies for Inclusive Growth

Inclusive growth can be pursued through a variety of strategies and interventions, including:

1. **Investments in Human Capital:** Investing in education, healthcare, and skills development is essential for promoting inclusive growth by enhancing human capital and productivity, reducing poverty and inequality, and empowering individuals to participate fully in the economy and society.

2. **Promotion of Decent Work:** Creating opportunities for decent and productive employment is essential for inclusive growth, as it provides individuals with a source of income, social protection, and dignity, while also contributing to economic growth and development.

3. **Social Protection Programs:** Social protection programs, such as cash transfers, food assistance, and healthcare subsidies, help to mitigate the impact of economic shocks and crises on vulnerable populations, while also promoting social inclusion and reducing poverty and inequality.

4. **Infrastructure Development:** Investments in infrastructure, such as roads, bridges, schools, and hospitals, are essential for promoting inclusive growth by improving access to essential services, reducing transportation costs, and facilitating economic activity in underserved areas.

5. **Financial Inclusion:** Promoting access to financial services, such as savings accounts, credit, insurance, and remittances, is critical for inclusive growth, as it enables individuals and households to invest in productive activities, build assets, and manage risks.

Challenges and Considerations

Inclusive growth faces several challenges and considerations, including:

1. **Structural Barriers:** Structural barriers, such as discrimination, exclusion, and lack of access to basic services, can hinder efforts to promote inclusive growth, particularly for marginalized and disadvantaged groups.

2. **Political Economy Constraints:** Political economy constraints, such as vested interests, rent-seeking behavior, and corruption, can undermine efforts to implement inclusive growth policies and reforms, and perpetuate patterns of inequality and exclusion.

3. **Environmental Degradation:** Environmental degradation and climate change pose significant challenges to inclusive growth, as they can exacerbate poverty, displacement, and vulnerability, particularly for communities dependent on natural resources for their livelihoods.

4. **Globalization and Technological Change:** Globalization and technological change can create winners and losers in the global economy, leading to increased inequality and job displacement, particularly for low-skilled workers and vulnerable populations.

Implications for Social Justice and Economic Prosperity

Inclusive growth has profound implications for social justice, economic prosperity, and sustainable development:

1. **Reducing Poverty and Inequality:** Inclusive growth helps to reduce poverty and inequality by expanding opportunities for income generation, improving access to essential services, and promoting social inclusion and mobility.

2. **Promoting Economic Stability:** Inclusive growth promotes economic stability by reducing social tensions and conflicts,

enhancing social cohesion and trust, and fostering a more resilient and adaptable economy.

3. **Fostering Innovation and Creativity:** Inclusive growth fosters innovation and creativity by harnessing the talents and potential of all members of society, regardless of their background or circumstances.

4. **Enhancing Global Competitiveness:** Inclusive growth enhances global competitiveness by promoting a skilled and healthy workforce, reducing social disparities and inefficiencies, and fostering a more dynamic and inclusive economy.

Inclusive growth is essential for promoting social justice, economic prosperity, and sustainable development. By prioritizing equity, opportunity, and sustainability, inclusive growth helps to reduce poverty and inequality, promote social cohesion and stability, and foster a more resilient and inclusive economy. While inclusive growth may face challenges and constraints, its benefits in terms of fostering human development, reducing social disparities, and promoting shared prosperity make it a crucial component of efforts to build a more just, equitable, and sustainable future for all. Through sustained commitment and collaboration among government, civil society, the private sector, and other stakeholders, inclusive growth can help to create a world where all individuals have the opportunity to thrive and fulfill their potential.

Social Safety Nets: Ensuring Economic Stability

Social safety nets are a crucial component of modern welfare states, providing essential support and protection to individuals and families facing economic hardship or vulnerability. These programs encompass a range of social assistance measures, including cash transfers, food assistance, unemployment benefits, healthcare coverage, and housing subsidies, among others. Social safety nets play a vital role in ensuring economic stability by mitigating the impact of economic shocks and crises, reducing poverty and inequality, and promoting social cohesion and resilience. In this exploration of social safety nets, we delve into their principles, functions, design considerations, challenges, and implications for fostering economic stability and social well-being.

Principles of Social Safety Nets

Social safety nets are guided by several key principles that shape their design and implementation:

1. **Universal Coverage:** Social safety nets aim to provide protection and support to all members of society, regardless of their income, employment status, or social background. By ensuring universal coverage, social safety nets help to prevent exclusion and ensure that no one falls through the cracks.

2. **Targeting:** While social safety nets aim to provide universal coverage, they also target assistance to those who are most in need. Targeting mechanisms, such as means testing, geographic targeting, or categorical targeting, help to ensure that resources are directed towards the most vulnerable and marginalized populations.

3. **Equity and Fairness:** Social safety nets prioritize equity and fairness by providing assistance based on need rather than merit or entitlement. They aim to reduce disparities in income, wealth, and opportunities, and promote social justice and solidarity among all members of society.

4. **Resilience and Adaptability:** Social safety nets are designed to be flexible and adaptable to changing economic and social conditions. They provide a buffer against economic shocks and crises, helping individuals and families to cope with adversity and rebuild their lives in times of need.

Functions of Social Safety Nets

Social safety nets serve several key functions in promoting economic stability and social well-being:

1. **Poverty Reduction:** Social safety nets help to reduce poverty by providing direct assistance and support to individuals and families facing economic hardship. Cash transfers, food assistance, and other social assistance measures help to ensure that basic needs are met and that individuals can access essential goods and services.

2. **Income Smoothing:** Social safety nets provide a cushion against income volatility and uncertainty, helping individuals and families to maintain a basic standard of living during periods of unemployment, illness, or other emergencies. Unemployment benefits, sickness benefits, and other income replacement programs help to smooth consumption and stabilize household finances.

3. **Human Capital Investment:** Social safety nets promote human capital investment by ensuring that individuals have access to education, healthcare, and other essential services. By reducing barriers to access and providing financial support, social safety nets help to ensure that all members of society can develop their skills, talents, and capabilities to their fullest potential.

4. **Social Cohesion:** Social safety nets foster social cohesion and solidarity by providing a sense of security and belonging to all members of society. By promoting equity, fairness, and social justice, social safety nets help to build trust and cooperation among individuals and communities, strengthening social bonds and resilience.

Design Considerations for Social Safety Nets

Designing effective social safety nets requires careful consideration of several key factors, including:

1. **Coverage and Targeting:** Social safety nets must strike a balance between universality and targeting, ensuring that assistance reaches those who are most in need without excluding others. Designing effective targeting mechanisms and eligibility criteria is essential to ensure that resources are directed towards the most vulnerable and marginalized populations.

2. **Benefit Levels and Duration:** Social safety nets must provide adequate levels of support to meet the basic needs of beneficiaries and enable them to maintain a decent standard of living. Setting appropriate benefit levels and duration of assistance is essential to ensure that social safety nets are effective in reducing poverty and inequality.

3. **Administrative Efficiency:** Social safety nets must be administratively efficient and cost-effective to ensure that resources are used efficiently and reach intended beneficiaries in a timely manner. Streamlining application procedures, reducing bureaucratic barriers, and leveraging technology can help to improve the efficiency and effectiveness of social safety net programs.

4. **Comprehensive Approach:** Social safety nets should take a comprehensive approach to addressing the multiple dimensions of poverty and vulnerability. This may involve integrating cash transfers with complementary services, such as healthcare, education, and vocational training, to provide holistic support to individuals and families facing economic hardship.

Challenges and Considerations

Social safety nets face several challenges and considerations, including:

1. **Fiscal Sustainability:** Funding social safety nets can be challenging, particularly in low- and middle-income countries with limited fiscal resources. Balancing the need for adequate social protection with fiscal sustainability requires careful planning, prioritization, and resource mobilization.

2. **Political Economy Constraints:** Social safety nets may face opposition from powerful vested interests who stand to lose from more redistributive policies. Overcoming political economy constraints and building public support for social safety nets requires effective advocacy, communication, and coalition-building.

3. **Administrative Capacity:** Implementing social safety nets requires strong administrative capacity to design, deliver, and monitor programs effectively. Strengthening institutional capacity, investing in staff training and development, and leveraging technology can help to improve the efficiency and effectiveness of social safety net programs.

4. **Social Stigma and Exclusion:** Social safety nets may be subject to social stigma and exclusion, particularly in contexts where beneficiaries are perceived as undeserving or dependent. Addressing social stigma and promoting social inclusion requires raising awareness, challenging stereotypes, and fostering empathy and solidarity among all members of society.

Implications for Economic Stability and Social Well-Being

Social safety nets have profound implications for economic stability and social well-being:

1. **Promoting Economic Stability:** Social safety nets help to stabilize the economy by reducing income volatility and uncertainty, maintaining aggregate demand, and mitigating the impact of economic shocks and crises on vulnerable populations.

2. **Reducing Poverty and Inequality:** Social safety nets help to reduce poverty and inequality by providing direct assistance and support to individuals and families facing economic hardship. By ensuring that basic needs are met and that all members of society have access to essential goods and services, social safety nets help to build a more equitable and inclusive economy.

3. **Fostering Social Cohesion:** Social safety nets foster social cohesion and solidarity by providing a sense of security and belonging to all members of society. By promoting equity, fairness, and social justice, social safety nets help to build trust and cooperation among individuals and communities, strengthening social bonds and resilience.

4. **Enhancing Human Development:** Social safety nets promote human development by ensuring that all individuals have access to education, healthcare, and other essential services. By reducing barriers to access and providing financial support, social safety nets help to ensure that all members of society can develop their skills, talents, and capabilities to their fullest potential.

Social safety nets are essential for ensuring economic stability, reducing poverty and inequality, and promoting social cohesion and well-being. By providing essential support and protection to individuals and families facing economic hardship or vulnerability, social safety nets help to build a more resilient, equitable, and inclusive society. While social safety nets may face challenges and constraints, their benefits in terms of fostering economic stability, social justice, and human development make them a crucial component of efforts to build a more just and sustainable future for all. Through sustained commitment and investment in social protection, societies can ensure that no one is left behind and that all members of society have the opportunity to thrive and fulfill their potential.

Chapter 10

Environmental Reconciliation: Finding Balance with Nature

Environmental reconciliation is a critical imperative in our modern world, as we grapple with the consequences of unsustainable exploitation of natural resources and the degradation of ecosystems. This chapter explores the urgent need to harmonize human activities with the natural world, recognizing the interconnectedness of environmental health and human well-being. Environmental reconciliation calls for a fundamental shift in our relationship with nature, moving towards practices that promote conservation, regeneration, and sustainable use of resources. In this exploration, we delve into the principles, challenges, and strategies for achieving environmental reconciliation, recognizing its significance for preserving biodiversity, mitigating climate change, and ensuring the long-term viability of our planet for future generations.

Conservation and Preservation Efforts: Sustaining Biodiversity and Ecosystem Health

Conservation and preservation efforts are essential components of environmental reconciliation, aiming to protect and restore the natural world's biodiversity and ecosystems. In the face of escalating environmental degradation and habitat loss, these efforts have become increasingly urgent. Conservation focuses on sustainable management practices to prevent further degradation and promote the recovery of ecosystems, while preservation aims to maintain natural areas in their pristine state, safeguarding biodiversity and ecological integrity. This chapter explores the principles, strategies, challenges, and implications of conservation and preservation efforts in fostering environmental reconciliation and ensuring the long-term sustainability of our planet's ecosystems.

Principles of Conservation and Preservation

Conservation and preservation efforts are guided by several key principles that underpin their approach to protecting and managing natural resources:

1. **Biodiversity Conservation:** Biodiversity is the foundation of healthy ecosystems, providing resilience and stability to natural systems. Conservation efforts prioritize the protection and restoration of biodiversity, recognizing the intrinsic value of species and ecosystems and their essential roles in supporting life on Earth.

2. **Ecosystem Integrity:** Ecosystems are complex, interconnected systems comprised of diverse species and habitats. Preservation efforts aim to maintain ecosystem integrity by protecting intact ecosystems and restoring degraded ones, ensuring that ecological processes continue to function effectively.

3. **Sustainable Resource Use:** Conservation practices promote the sustainable use of natural resources, balancing human needs with the need to maintain ecosystem health and integrity. This involves adopting practices that minimize environmental impact, reduce waste, and promote resource efficiency.

4. **Community Engagement:** Conservation and preservation efforts recognize the importance of engaging local communities and indigenous peoples in decision-making processes and management initiatives. Empowering local communities to take ownership of conservation efforts fosters a sense of stewardship and ensures that conservation practices are culturally appropriate and socially equitable.

Strategies for Conservation and Preservation

Conservation and preservation efforts employ a variety of strategies and interventions to protect and restore ecosystems and biodiversity:

1. **Protected Areas:** Protected areas, such as national parks, wildlife reserves, and marine sanctuaries, play a crucial role in conserving biodiversity and preserving natural habitats. These areas provide safe havens for wildlife, regulate ecosystem services, and offer opportunities for scientific research, education, and ecotourism.

2. **Habitat Restoration:** Habitat restoration involves the rehabilitation of degraded ecosystems to improve biodiversity and ecological function. Restoration efforts may include reforestation, wetland restoration, coral reef rehabilitation, and reintroduction of native species, among others.

3. **Sustainable Land Management:** Sustainable land management practices aim to promote land use practices that conserve soil, water, and biodiversity while supporting agricultural productivity and rural livelihoods. These practices include agroforestry, organic farming, soil conservation, and integrated watershed management.

4. **Wildlife Conservation:** Wildlife conservation efforts focus on protecting endangered species, conserving critical habitats, and addressing threats such as poaching, habitat loss, and human-wildlife conflict. Conservation measures may include habitat protection, captive breeding programs, anti-poaching patrols, and community-based conservation initiatives.

5. **Marine Conservation:** Marine conservation efforts aim to protect and restore ocean ecosystems, including coral reefs, mangroves, and seagrass beds. Conservation measures may

include marine protected areas, sustainable fisheries management, coastal zone management, and marine pollution control.

Challenges and Considerations

Conservation and preservation efforts face several challenges and considerations, including:

1. **Habitat Fragmentation:** Habitat fragmentation and loss due to urbanization, agriculture, infrastructure development, and deforestation pose significant threats to biodiversity and ecosystem health. Addressing habitat fragmentation requires landscape-level conservation planning and coordination across multiple stakeholders and sectors.

2. **Climate Change:** Climate change exacerbates existing threats to biodiversity and ecosystems, altering habitats, disrupting ecological processes, and increasing the frequency and intensity of extreme weather events. Conservation efforts must adapt to changing environmental conditions and incorporate climate resilience into management practices.

3. **Invasive Species:** Invasive species pose a major threat to native biodiversity, outcompeting native species, disrupting ecosystems, and altering ecological processes. Controlling invasive species requires coordinated management efforts, including surveillance, eradication, and prevention measures.

4. **Resource Extraction:** Unsustainable resource extraction, including logging, mining, and industrial agriculture, contributes to habitat destruction, pollution, and loss of biodiversity. Balancing economic development with conservation requires implementing sustainable resource management practices and promoting alternative livelihoods.

Implications for Environmental Reconciliation

Conservation and preservation efforts have profound implications for environmental reconciliation and the long-term sustainability of our planet:

1. **Biodiversity Conservation:** Protecting and restoring biodiversity is essential for maintaining ecosystem resilience, supporting ecosystem services, and safeguarding the planet's capacity to support life.

2. **Ecosystem Health:** Preserving intact ecosystems and restoring degraded ones helps to maintain ecosystem integrity, regulate climate, purify air and water, and provide habitat for wildlife.

3. **Human Well-Being:** Healthy ecosystems contribute to human well-being by providing essential goods and services, including food, clean water, medicines, and recreational opportunities.

4. **Cultural and Spiritual Values:** Conservation and preservation efforts help to protect cultural and spiritual values associated with natural areas, including traditional knowledge, cultural heritage, and sacred sites.

Conservation and preservation efforts are essential for protecting and restoring biodiversity, preserving ecosystem integrity, and fostering environmental reconciliation. By adopting sustainable land management practices, establishing protected areas, restoring degraded habitats, and addressing threats such as climate change and invasive species, we can ensure that ecosystems continue to thrive and provide essential benefits to both humans and nature. Through collaboration, innovation, and collective action, we can build a more sustainable and resilient future for generations to come, where humans and nature coexist in harmony and mutual respect.

Sustainable Development: Balancing Growth and Preservation

Sustainable development is a holistic approach to addressing the interconnected challenges of economic growth, social equity, and environmental conservation. It recognizes that human well-being depends on the health of the planet and seeks to meet the needs of the present without compromising the ability of future generations to meet their own needs. At its core, sustainable development aims to balance economic prosperity, social progress, and environmental protection to ensure a more equitable and resilient future for all. In this exploration of sustainable development, we delve into its principles, strategies, challenges, and implications for fostering environmental reconciliation and promoting the long-term well-being of humanity and the planet.

Principles of Sustainable Development

Sustainable development is guided by several key principles that shape its approach to achieving a harmonious balance between economic, social, and environmental objectives:

1. **Interdependence:** Sustainable development recognizes the interconnectedness of human activities and the natural world, understanding that economic prosperity, social well-being, and environmental health are mutually dependent and interrelated.

2. **Equity and Social Justice:** Sustainable development prioritizes social equity and inclusion, ensuring that the benefits of development are shared equitably among all members of society, particularly the most vulnerable and marginalized.

3. **Environmental Integrity:** Sustainable development seeks to protect and restore the health of the planet's ecosystems, recognizing that ecological sustainability is essential for supporting human life and well-being.

4. **Precautionary Approach:** Sustainable development adopts a precautionary approach to decision-making, recognizing that uncertainty and complexity are inherent in environmental and social systems. This involves taking proactive measures to prevent harm and mitigate risks, even in the absence of conclusive scientific evidence.

Strategies for Sustainable Development

Sustainable development encompasses a range of strategies and interventions aimed at promoting economic prosperity, social progress, and environmental protection:

1. **Green Growth:** Green growth focuses on decoupling economic growth from environmental degradation by promoting resource efficiency, innovation, and sustainable consumption and production patterns. This involves investing in clean technologies, renewable energy, and green infrastructure to foster economic development while minimizing environmental impact.

2. **Poverty Alleviation:** Sustainable development aims to eradicate poverty and reduce inequality by promoting inclusive economic growth, expanding access to education, healthcare, and social services, and empowering marginalized and vulnerable groups.

3. **Environmental Conservation:** Sustainable development prioritizes environmental conservation and biodiversity protection, safeguarding critical habitats, and ecosystems, and restoring degraded lands and waters. This involves establishing protected areas, implementing sustainable land and water management practices, and combating threats such as deforestation, pollution, and habitat loss.

4. **Community Engagement:** Sustainable development engages local communities and indigenous peoples as partners in decision-making and development initiatives, respecting their rights, knowledge, and cultural heritage, and fostering participatory approaches to planning and implementation.

Challenges and Considerations

Sustainable development faces several challenges and considerations, including:

1. **Trade-offs and Conflicts:** Balancing economic, social, and environmental objectives can be challenging, as they often involve trade-offs and conflicts between competing interests and priorities. Achieving consensus and reconciling divergent perspectives requires dialogue, negotiation, and compromise among stakeholders.

2. **Short-termism:** Short-term economic interests and political considerations may prioritize immediate gains over long-term sustainability, leading to unsustainable resource exploitation, environmental degradation, and social inequality. Overcoming short-termism requires political leadership, public awareness, and institutional reforms that prioritize the long-term well-being of society and the planet.

3. **Globalization and Consumption Patterns:** Globalization and unsustainable consumption patterns exacerbate environmental degradation and social inequality, placing increasing pressure on finite natural resources and ecosystems. Shifting towards more sustainable consumption and production patterns, reducing waste and pollution, and promoting resource efficiency are essential for achieving sustainable development.

4. **Climate Change:** Climate change poses a significant threat to sustainable development, with profound implications for

ecosystems, economies, and societies worldwide. Mitigating climate change requires ambitious emission reduction targets, adaptation measures, and international cooperation to transition to a low-carbon, resilient economy.

Implications for Environmental Reconciliation

Sustainable development has profound implications for environmental reconciliation and the long-term sustainability of our planet:

1. **Promoting Environmental Reconciliation:** Sustainable development fosters environmental reconciliation by promoting the harmonious coexistence of human activities and the natural world. By integrating environmental conservation, social equity, and economic prosperity, sustainable development helps to address the root causes of environmental degradation and promote a more balanced and sustainable relationship with nature.

2. **Ensuring Resilience and Adaptation:** Sustainable development builds resilience and adaptive capacity to environmental change, helping communities and ecosystems to withstand and recover from shocks and disturbances. By promoting diversity, flexibility, and innovation, sustainable development enhances the ability of societies and ecosystems to adapt to changing environmental conditions.

3. **Fostering Collaboration and Partnership:** Sustainable development fosters collaboration and partnership among governments, civil society, the private sector, and other stakeholders to address shared environmental challenges and achieve common goals. By promoting dialogue, cooperation, and collective action, sustainable development enhances the effectiveness and impact of environmental reconciliation efforts.

4. **Empowering Future Generations:** Sustainable development ensures that future generations inherit a planet that is healthy, resilient, and sustainable. By integrating long-term thinking, intergenerational equity, and stewardship into decision-making processes and development initiatives, sustainable development empowers future generations to live in harmony with nature and enjoy a high quality of life.

Sustainable development offers a holistic and integrated approach to addressing the complex challenges of our time, balancing economic growth, social equity, and environmental protection to ensure a more equitable and sustainable future for all. By embracing the principles of interdependence, equity, environmental integrity, and precautionary action, sustainable development fosters environmental reconciliation and promotes the long-term well-being of humanity and the planet. Through collaboration, innovation, and collective action, we can build a more resilient, inclusive, and sustainable world where people and nature thrive in harmony and balance.

Climate Change Mitigation: Global Efforts for Environmental Harmony

Climate change mitigation is a critical imperative in the face of escalating global warming and its far-reaching impacts on ecosystems, economies, and societies worldwide. It entails reducing greenhouse gas emissions and enhancing carbon sinks to limit the magnitude and rate of climate change, thereby mitigating its adverse effects on the environment and human well-being. This chapter explores the urgent need for coordinated global efforts to address climate change, examining the principles, strategies, challenges, and implications of climate change mitigation for fostering environmental harmony and ensuring the long-term sustainability of our planet.

Principles of Climate Change Mitigation

Climate change mitigation is guided by several key principles that underpin its approach to reducing greenhouse gas emissions and enhancing resilience to climate change:

1. **Precautionary Principle:** Climate change mitigation adopts a precautionary approach to decision-making, recognizing the uncertainties and risks associated with global warming and its impacts. It emphasizes the need for proactive measures to prevent dangerous levels of climate change, even in the absence of full scientific certainty.

2. **Common but Differentiated Responsibility:** Climate change mitigation recognizes that all countries share a common responsibility to address climate change, but that their contributions should be differentiated based on historical emissions, current emissions levels, and development needs. It emphasizes the importance of equity, fairness, and shared commitment in international climate action.

3. **Sustainability:** Climate change mitigation promotes sustainability by aligning economic development with environmental protection and social equity. It seeks to decouple economic growth from greenhouse gas emissions, promote resource efficiency, and foster a transition to a low-carbon, resilient economy.

4. **Interconnectedness:** Climate change mitigation recognizes the interconnectedness of environmental, social, and economic systems, understanding that actions taken to reduce greenhouse gas emissions can have co-benefits for human health, biodiversity conservation, and sustainable development.

Strategies for Climate Change Mitigation

Climate change mitigation encompasses a range of strategies and interventions aimed at reducing greenhouse gas emissions and enhancing resilience to climate change:

1. **Transition to Renewable Energy:** Transitioning to renewable energy sources, such as solar, wind, hydroelectric, and geothermal power, is essential for reducing reliance on fossil fuels and decreasing greenhouse gas emissions from the energy sector. This involves investing in renewable energy infrastructure, improving energy efficiency, and phasing out subsidies for fossil fuels.

2. **Energy Efficiency:** Improving energy efficiency in buildings, transportation, industry, and agriculture is critical for reducing energy consumption and greenhouse gas emissions. This involves implementing energy-saving technologies, improving building codes and standards, and promoting behavioral changes to reduce energy use.

3. **Sustainable Land Use:** Sustainable land use practices, such as afforestation, reforestation, agroforestry, and sustainable agriculture, help to enhance carbon sequestration and reduce emissions from deforestation and land degradation. This involves protecting forests, restoring degraded lands, and promoting sustainable land management practices that conserve soil, water, and biodiversity.

4. **Emissions Reduction Targets:** Setting ambitious emissions reduction targets and implementing policies and regulations to achieve them is essential for driving emissions reductions across all sectors of the economy. This involves implementing carbon pricing mechanisms, such as carbon taxes or cap-and-trade systems, and incentivizing emission reductions through subsidies, grants, and other financial mechanisms.

5. **Climate Resilience:** Enhancing climate resilience and adaptation is essential for reducing vulnerability to climate change impacts, such as extreme weather events, sea-level rise, and water scarcity. This involves investing in climate-resilient infrastructure, strengthening early warning systems, and promoting ecosystem-based approaches to adaptation.

Challenges and Considerations

Climate change mitigation faces several challenges and considerations, including:

1. **Political Will:** Climate change mitigation requires strong political leadership and commitment at the national and international levels to overcome vested interests, political inertia, and short-term economic considerations. Building consensus and mobilizing support for ambitious climate action requires effective communication, advocacy, and public engagement.

2. **Technological Innovation:** Climate change mitigation relies on technological innovation and research and development to develop low-carbon technologies, improve energy efficiency, and enhance climate resilience. Investing in research, development, and deployment of clean energy technologies is essential for achieving emissions reductions at scale.

3. **Finance and Investment:** Climate change mitigation requires substantial financial resources to support emissions reductions, adaptation measures, and technology transfer to developing countries. Mobilizing climate finance from public and private sources, as well as leveraging innovative financing mechanisms, such as green bonds and climate funds, is essential for scaling up climate action.

4. **International Cooperation:** Climate change mitigation requires international cooperation and collaboration to address

global emissions and support vulnerable countries in adapting to climate change impacts. Strengthening multilateral institutions, enhancing transparency and accountability, and fostering partnerships between governments, civil society, and the private sector are essential for achieving effective and equitable climate action.

Implications for Environmental Harmony

Climate change mitigation has profound implications for environmental harmony and the long-term sustainability of our planet:

1. **Protecting Ecosystems:** Climate change mitigation helps to protect ecosystems and biodiversity by reducing emissions of greenhouse gases and enhancing resilience to climate change impacts. By preserving habitats, conserving biodiversity, and restoring degraded lands, climate change mitigation contributes to environmental harmony and ecosystem health.

2. **Safeguarding Human Health:** Climate change mitigation has co-benefits for human health by reducing air and water pollution, improving air quality, and promoting active transportation and sustainable lifestyles. By addressing the root causes of climate change, such as fossil fuel combustion and deforestation, climate change mitigation helps to create healthier and more livable communities.

3. **Promoting Social Equity:** Climate change mitigation promotes social equity by addressing the disproportionate impacts of climate change on vulnerable and marginalized communities, such as low-income households, indigenous peoples, and frontline communities. By prioritizing equity, fairness, and social justice, climate change mitigation fosters environmental harmony and social cohesion.

4. **Fostering Economic Prosperity:** Climate change mitigation drives innovation, creates jobs, and stimulates economic growth in clean energy, sustainable transportation, and green infrastructure sectors. By investing in renewable energy, energy efficiency, and climate-resilient infrastructure, climate change mitigation fosters economic prosperity and long-term competitiveness.

Climate change mitigation is essential for addressing the urgent threat of global warming and promoting environmental harmony and sustainability. By reducing greenhouse gas emissions, enhancing resilience to climate change impacts, and promoting sustainable development pathways, climate change mitigation helps to protect ecosystems, safeguard human health, promote social equity, and foster economic prosperity. Through coordinated global efforts, political leadership, and collective action, we can build a more resilient, equitable, and sustainable future for all, where people and nature thrive in harmony and balance.

Chapter 11
Technological Solutions: Tools for Unity in the Digital Age

In the digital age, technological advancements have transformed the way we communicate, collaborate, and address global challenges. From artificial intelligence and blockchain to virtual reality and renewable energy technologies, innovations are shaping the future of humanity and offering unprecedented opportunities for unity and cooperation. This chapter explores the role of technological solutions as tools for fostering unity and addressing pressing global issues. By harnessing the power of technology, we can overcome barriers, bridge divides, and create a more interconnected and harmonious world. In this exploration, we delve into the principles, applications, challenges, and implications of technological solutions in promoting unity, sustainability, and prosperity in the digital age.

Leveraging Technology for Connection

In today's interconnected world, technology plays a crucial role in facilitating connections and fostering unity among individuals, communities, and societies. From social media platforms and messaging apps to video conferencing and virtual reality, technological innovations have revolutionized the way we communicate, collaborate, and interact with one another. This chapter explores how we can leverage technology to build connections, bridge divides, and promote unity in an increasingly digitalized world. By harnessing the power of technology for connection, we can overcome geographical barriers, cultural differences, and social isolation, creating a more inclusive and harmonious global community.

The Power of Connectivity

Technology has transformed the way we connect with one another, enabling instant communication and collaboration across vast distances. Social media platforms, such as Facebook, Twitter, and Instagram, allow us to share ideas, experiences, and perspectives with friends, family, and colleagues around the world. Messaging apps, such as WhatsApp, WeChat, and Telegram, enable real-time communication and coordination, facilitating seamless interactions across borders and time zones. Video conferencing tools, such as Zoom, Skype, and Google Meet, enable face-to-face communication and collaboration, fostering a sense of presence and connection even in virtual environments.

Building Virtual Communities

Technology has enabled the creation of virtual communities, bringing together like-minded individuals and interest groups from diverse backgrounds and locations. Online forums, discussion boards, and social networking sites provide platforms for people to connect, share information, and engage in meaningful conversations on topics ranging from hobbies and interests to professional expertise and social causes. Virtual communities offer opportunities for individuals to find support, seek advice, and build relationships with others who share their passions and values, fostering a sense of belonging and solidarity in an increasingly fragmented world.

Breaking Down Barriers

Technology has the potential to break down barriers and promote understanding and empathy across cultural, linguistic, and geographical divides. Translation tools and language learning apps help facilitate communication and comprehension between speakers of different languages, enabling people to engage in cross-cultural dialogue and exchange. Virtual reality experiences and immersive storytelling platforms offer opportunities for people to step into each other's shoes and gain new perspectives on the world, fostering empathy and compassion for others' lived experiences.

Addressing Social Isolation

Technology can help address social isolation and loneliness by providing avenues for social connection and support, particularly for marginalized and vulnerable populations. Online support groups, peer-to-peer networks, and mental health apps offer resources and community for individuals struggling with loneliness, depression, and anxiety, providing a lifeline of support and solidarity in times of need. Telemedicine and remote counseling services enable individuals to access healthcare and mental health support from the comfort and safety of their own homes, reducing barriers to care and promoting well-being.

Challenges and Considerations

While technology offers immense potential for connection and unity, it also presents challenges and considerations that must be addressed:

1. **Digital Divide:** The digital divide, characterized by disparities in access to and use of technology, remains a significant barrier to connectivity and inclusion, particularly in low-income communities and rural areas. Bridging the digital divide requires efforts to expand access to affordable internet connectivity, devices, and digital literacy training, ensuring that everyone has the opportunity to benefit from technology's potential for connection.

2. **Privacy and Security:** The widespread use of technology raises concerns about privacy and security, particularly in relation to personal data and online interactions. Protecting individuals'

privacy and safeguarding against cyber threats, such as hacking, phishing, and identity theft, requires robust cybersecurity measures, transparent data practices, and informed consent mechanisms to ensure trust and confidence in digital platforms.

3. **Digital Exhaustion:** The constant connectivity and information overload facilitated by technology can lead to digital exhaustion and burnout, negatively impacting mental health and well-being. Balancing online and offline activities, setting boundaries around technology use, and practicing mindfulness and self-care are essential for maintaining a healthy relationship with technology and fostering sustainable connections.

4. **Echo Chambers and Polarization:** Social media algorithms and filter bubbles can contribute to the formation of echo chambers and polarization, reinforcing existing beliefs and isolating individuals from diverse perspectives. Promoting digital literacy, critical thinking, and media literacy skills is essential for navigating online spaces and engaging in constructive dialogue across ideological divides, fostering understanding and mutual respect.

Implications for Unity and Connection

Leveraging technology for connection has profound implications for promoting unity, empathy, and collaboration in an increasingly interconnected world:

1. **Fostering Inclusivity:** Technology enables us to reach across borders and boundaries to connect with others, fostering inclusivity and diversity in our communities and societies. By providing platforms for voices to be heard and stories to be shared, technology empowers individuals to participate in shaping their collective futures and promoting social justice and equality.

2. **Empowering Communities:** Technology empowers communities to organize, mobilize, and advocate for social change, amplifying voices and catalyzing collective action around shared values and goals. By providing tools for grassroots organizing and civic engagement, technology strengthens civil society and promotes democratic participation, fostering a sense of agency and empowerment among citizens.

3. **Cultivating Empathy:** Technology has the potential to cultivate empathy and compassion by exposing us to diverse perspectives and lived experiences. Through virtual reality simulations, immersive storytelling, and interactive media, we can step into each other's shoes and gain a deeper understanding of the human condition, fostering empathy and solidarity across cultural, social, and ideological divides.

4. **Building Resilient Communities:** Technology can help build resilient communities and societies by facilitating communication, collaboration, and coordination in times of crisis and uncertainty. From natural disasters and public health emergencies to social unrest and political upheaval, technology enables individuals and organizations to mobilize resources, disseminate information, and provide support to those in need, strengthening social cohesion and resilience in the face of adversity.

Leveraging technology for connection offers immense opportunities for building unity, empathy, and collaboration in an increasingly digitalized world. By harnessing the power of technology to overcome barriers, bridge divides, and promote understanding and solidarity

Digital Diplomacy: Online Platforms for Harmony

In today's interconnected world, diplomacy has evolved beyond traditional channels of communication to encompass a digital dimension. Digital diplomacy leverages online platforms, social media, and digital tools to facilitate dialogue, build relationships, and promote cooperation among nations, organizations, and individuals. This chapter explores the role of digital diplomacy in fostering harmony and addressing global challenges in the digital age. By harnessing the power of technology and online platforms, digital diplomacy offers unprecedented opportunities for dialogue, collaboration, and conflict resolution, creating pathways for unity and cooperation in an increasingly complex and interconnected world.

The Emergence of Digital Diplomacy

Digital diplomacy has emerged as a response to the rapid expansion of digital technologies and the increasing importance of online communication in international relations. Diplomatic missions, government agencies, and international organizations have embraced digital platforms, such as social media, websites, and online forums, to engage with foreign audiences, disseminate information, and influence public opinion. Digital diplomacy complements traditional diplomatic practices by providing new channels for communication, outreach, and engagement, expanding the reach and impact of diplomatic efforts in the digital age.

Engagement and Dialogue

Digital diplomacy facilitates engagement and dialogue between governments, diplomats, and citizens, fostering transparency, accountability, and inclusivity in diplomatic processes. Social media platforms, such as Twitter, Facebook, and Instagram, enable diplomats to engage directly with foreign audiences, share information, and respond to inquiries in real-time, breaking down barriers and building trust. Online forums and virtual events provide opportunities for diplomatic dialogues, track-two diplomacy, and public diplomacy initiatives, bringing together diverse stakeholders to discuss pressing issues and explore solutions collaboratively.

Crisis Communication and Conflict Resolution

Digital diplomacy plays a critical role in crisis communication and conflict resolution by providing channels for rapid response, crisis management, and de-escalation. During times of crisis, such as natural disasters, public health emergencies, or political unrest, digital platforms enable governments and international organizations to disseminate timely information, coordinate relief efforts, and provide assistance to affected populations. Digital tools, such as crisis mapping, crowdsourcing, and social media monitoring, help track developments on the ground, identify emerging risks, and mobilize resources to address urgent needs, mitigating the impact of crises and promoting stability and resilience.

Cultural Exchange and Soft Power

Digital diplomacy promotes cultural exchange and soft power projection by showcasing a country's culture, values, and achievements to international audiences. Cultural diplomacy initiatives, such as virtual exhibitions, online festivals, and digital storytelling projects, enable countries to share their cultural heritage and promote mutual understanding and appreciation among diverse communities. Social media influencers, digital content creators, and online ambassadors serve as cultural ambassadors, amplifying positive narratives and shaping perceptions of countries and cultures in the digital sphere, enhancing their soft power and influence on the global stage.

Challenges and Considerations

While digital diplomacy offers numerous benefits and opportunities, it also presents challenges and considerations that must be addressed:

1. **Disinformation and Misinformation:** The proliferation of disinformation and misinformation on digital platforms poses a significant challenge to digital diplomacy, undermining trust, distorting perceptions, and fueling conflict and division. Diplomats and governments must navigate complex information ecosystems, counter false narratives, and promote credible sources of information to combat misinformation effectively and protect the integrity of diplomatic communication.

2. **Digital Divide:** The digital divide, characterized by disparities in access to and use of digital technologies, limits the reach and impact of digital diplomacy initiatives, particularly in low-income countries and marginalized communities. Bridging the digital divide requires efforts to expand access to affordable internet connectivity, digital literacy training, and technology infrastructure, ensuring that everyone can participate in digital diplomacy efforts and benefit from their potential for engagement and empowerment.

3. **Privacy and Security:** Digital diplomacy raises concerns about privacy and security, particularly in relation to data protection, surveillance, and cybersecurity threats. Diplomatic missions and government agencies must adopt robust cybersecurity measures, encryption protocols, and data protection policies to safeguard sensitive information and ensure the confidentiality and integrity of diplomatic communications. Promoting transparency, accountability, and responsible data practices is essential for building trust and confidence in digital diplomacy initiatives and platforms.

4. **Ethical Considerations:** Digital diplomacy raises ethical considerations related to online behavior, diplomatic norms, and cultural sensitivities. Diplomats and government officials must adhere to ethical guidelines and diplomatic protocols when engaging on digital platforms, respecting local customs, laws, and regulations, and upholding principles of professionalism, integrity, and respect for human rights. Promoting ethical conduct and responsible engagement in digital diplomacy is essential for building trust and credibility with foreign audiences and fostering constructive dialogue and cooperation.

Implications for Harmony and Cooperation

Digital diplomacy has profound implications for fostering harmony, cooperation, and mutual understanding in the digital age:

1. **Building Bridges:** Digital diplomacy builds bridges between nations, cultures, and communities, fostering dialogue, cooperation, and mutual understanding across borders and boundaries. By providing platforms for engagement and exchange, digital diplomacy creates opportunities for building trust, resolving conflicts, and advancing shared interests and values, promoting harmony and stability in the international community.

2. **Enhancing Diplomatic Outreach:** Digital diplomacy enhances diplomatic outreach and engagement by expanding the reach and impact of diplomatic efforts beyond traditional channels of communication. Through social media, websites, and online forums, diplomats can engage directly with foreign audiences, amplify their messages, and build relationships with key stakeholders, enhancing the effectiveness and relevance of diplomatic initiatives and interventions.

3. **Promoting Public Diplomacy:** Digital diplomacy promotes public diplomacy by engaging with citizens, civil society

organizations, and non-state actors to advance common goals and values. By leveraging digital platforms for public outreach, cultural exchange, and people-to-people connections, diplomats can foster goodwill, promote positive perceptions, and build enduring relationships with foreign publics, enhancing mutual trust and cooperation between countries and communities.

4. **Empowering Citizens:** Digital diplomacy empowers citizens to participate in diplomatic processes, hold governments accountable, and contribute to global decision-making. Through social media campaigns, online petitions, and digital advocacy initiatives, citizens can mobilize support for diplomatic initiatives, raise awareness about pressing issues, and influence policy outcomes, fostering a more inclusive and democratic approach to international relations.

Digital diplomacy offers unprecedented opportunities for fostering harmony, cooperation, and mutual understanding in an increasingly interconnected and digitalized world. By leveraging technology and online platforms, diplomats can engage with foreign audiences, promote dialogue, and advance shared goals and values, transcending geographical, cultural, and political boundaries. Through thoughtful engagement, responsible communication, and strategic collaboration, digital diplomacy has the potential to build bridges, bridge divides, and create pathways for unity and cooperation in the pursuit of a more peaceful, prosperous, and sustainable future for all.

Artificial Intelligence for Conflict Resolution

Artificial intelligence (AI) has emerged as a powerful tool for addressing complex societal challenges, including conflict resolution and peacebuilding. By leveraging advanced algorithms, machine learning techniques, and big data analytics, AI systems can analyze vast amounts of information, identify patterns, and generate insights to support decision-making and intervention strategies in conflict-affected contexts. This chapter explores the potential of artificial intelligence for conflict resolution, examining its applications, benefits, challenges, and ethical considerations. From early warning systems and predictive analytics to mediation support and peacebuilding initiatives, AI offers innovative approaches to promoting peace, stability, and reconciliation in regions affected by conflict and violence.

Early Warning and Prediction

One of the key applications of artificial intelligence in conflict resolution is early warning and prediction of potential conflicts and violence. AI systems can analyze various data sources, including social media, news reports, satellite imagery, and sensor data, to identify early indicators of conflict, such as rising tensions, hate speech, and mass mobilization. By detecting patterns and anomalies in data, AI algorithms can generate real-time alerts and predictions, enabling policymakers, peacebuilders, and humanitarian actors to anticipate and prevent outbreaks of violence before they escalate.

Mediation and Negotiation Support

Artificial intelligence can also support mediation and negotiation processes by providing decision support tools, conflict analysis, and scenario planning capabilities. AI systems can analyze historical data on past conflicts, peace agreements, and negotiation outcomes to identify common patterns, strategies, and potential solutions. By simulating different negotiation scenarios and assessing their likely outcomes, AI algorithms can help mediators and negotiators develop informed strategies, prioritize issues, and identify areas of common ground, facilitating dialogue and consensus-building among conflicting parties.

Resource Allocation and Intervention Planning

Artificial intelligence can assist in resource allocation and intervention planning by optimizing the deployment of limited resources, such as humanitarian aid, peacekeeping forces, and development assistance. AI algorithms can analyze data on conflict dynamics, population movements, and humanitarian needs to identify priority areas for intervention and allocate resources based on risk and vulnerability assessments. By optimizing resource allocation and coordination among stakeholders, AI can maximize the impact and effectiveness of peacebuilding and humanitarian efforts, ensuring that assistance reaches those most in need.

Monitoring and Evaluation

Artificial intelligence can enhance monitoring and evaluation of peacebuilding and conflict resolution initiatives by providing real-time data collection, analysis, and feedback mechanisms. AI systems can analyze data on program activities, outcomes, and impact indicators to assess the effectiveness of interventions and identify lessons learned. By automating data collection and analysis processes, AI algorithms can provide timely insights and recommendations for improving program design, implementation, and impact, enhancing accountability and learning in the field of peacebuilding.

Challenges and Ethical Considerations

While artificial intelligence offers significant potential for conflict resolution, it also raises important challenges and ethical considerations that must be addressed:

1. **Bias and Fairness:** AI algorithms may perpetuate or amplify biases present in the data used to train them, leading to unfair or discriminatory outcomes, particularly in conflict-affected contexts characterized by social and political inequalities. Ensuring fairness and equity in AI systems requires careful

attention to data selection, algorithm design, and model validation, as well as transparency and accountability mechanisms to address bias and mitigate its impact on decision-making.

2. **Privacy and Security:** AI systems may pose risks to privacy and security, particularly in conflict-affected contexts where data collection and analysis may infringe on individuals' rights to privacy and confidentiality. Safeguarding sensitive information and ensuring data protection are essential for maintaining trust and legitimacy in AI-driven conflict resolution efforts, requiring robust data governance frameworks, encryption protocols, and informed consent mechanisms to protect the rights and interests of affected populations.

3. **Accountability and Transparency:** AI systems may lack transparency and accountability, making it difficult to understand how decisions are made and who is responsible for their outcomes. Establishing clear guidelines, standards, and mechanisms for accountability and transparency in AI-driven conflict resolution efforts is essential for ensuring trust, credibility, and legitimacy, enabling stakeholders to understand, challenge, and address potential biases, errors, or unintended consequences of AI algorithms.

4. **Human-Machine Interaction:** AI systems may raise concerns about the role of humans in decision-making processes and the potential for automation to replace or marginalize human agency and judgment in conflict resolution efforts. Balancing the benefits of automation with the need for human oversight, judgment, and intervention is essential for ensuring that AI complements rather than replaces human expertise, experience, and ethical judgment in the pursuit of peace and reconciliation.

Implications for Conflict Resolution

Artificial intelligence has profound implications for conflict resolution, offering new opportunities for preventing, managing, and resolving conflicts in an increasingly complex and interconnected world:

1. **Early Prevention:** By providing early warning and prediction capabilities, AI can help prevent conflicts before they escalate, enabling timely intervention and mediation efforts to address underlying grievances, mitigate tensions, and promote dialogue and reconciliation among conflicting parties.

2. **Informed Decision-Making:** By providing decision support tools and analysis, AI can assist policymakers, peacebuilders, and humanitarian actors in making informed decisions and prioritizing interventions based on data-driven insights and evidence, enhancing the effectiveness and impact of conflict resolution efforts.

3. **Collaborative Solutions:** By facilitating dialogue, negotiation, and consensus-building, AI can support collaborative approaches to conflict resolution, enabling conflicting parties to identify shared interests, explore mutually acceptable solutions, and work together towards sustainable peace and stability.

4. **Learning and Adaptation:** By providing monitoring and evaluation capabilities, AI can facilitate learning and adaptation in conflict resolution efforts, enabling stakeholders to assess the effectiveness of interventions, identify best practices, and adapt strategies based on real-time feedback and lessons learned, enhancing the agility and responsiveness of peacebuilding initiatives.

Artificial intelligence holds significant promise for conflict resolution, offering innovative approaches to preventing, managing, and resolving conflicts in an increasingly interconnected and digitalized world. By harnessing the power of AI for early warning and prediction, mediation and negotiation support, resource allocation and intervention planning, and monitoring and evaluation, we can enhance the effectiveness, efficiency, and impact of peacebuilding and conflict resolution efforts, promoting peace, stability, and reconciliation in regions affected by conflict and violence. However, addressing the challenges and ethical considerations raised by AI-driven conflict resolution requires careful attention to bias, privacy, accountability, and human-machine interaction, ensuring that AI complements rather than undermines human agency, judgment, and ethical values in the pursuit of peace and justice for all.

Chapter 12

Education for Unity: Nurturing Harmony in Future Generations

Education plays a pivotal role in shaping the values, attitudes, and behaviors of individuals and societies, laying the foundation for social cohesion, mutual respect, and peaceful coexistence. In an increasingly diverse and interconnected world, the need for education for unity and harmony has never been more critical. This chapter explores the importance of education in fostering unity, understanding, and empathy among future generations, examining the principles, practices, and challenges of promoting harmony through education. By nurturing inclusive classrooms, promoting intercultural dialogue, and teaching critical thinking and conflict resolution skills, education has the power to cultivate a culture of peace and tolerance, empowering young people to become active global citizens committed to building a more just, equitable, and harmonious world.

Teaching Conflict Resolution Skills

Conflict is an inevitable aspect of human interaction, arising from differences in opinions, values, and interests. However, conflicts can also provide opportunities for growth, learning, and relationship-building when managed effectively. In today's interconnected world, where diversity and globalization bring people from different backgrounds and perspectives together, teaching conflict resolution skills is essential for fostering harmony, cooperation, and understanding. This chapter explores the importance of teaching conflict resolution skills in educational settings, examining strategies, approaches, and best practices for equipping students with the tools they need to navigate conflicts constructively and contribute to a more peaceful and harmonious society.

Understanding Conflict

Before delving into conflict resolution skills, it is essential to understand the nature and dynamics of conflict. Conflict arises when individuals or groups perceive a divergence of interests, needs, or values, leading to tensions, disagreements, and disputes. Conflicts can manifest in various forms, including interpersonal conflicts between individuals, intergroup conflicts between communities or organizations, and intrapersonal conflicts within oneself. Understanding the root causes, triggers, and manifestations of conflict is crucial for effectively managing and resolving conflicts in educational settings and beyond.

The Importance of Conflict Resolution Skills

Teaching conflict resolution skills is essential for several reasons:

1. **Promoting Peaceful Coexistence:** Conflict resolution skills empower individuals to address conflicts peacefully and constructively, reducing the likelihood of escalation and violence. By teaching students how to manage conflicts through dialogue, negotiation, and compromise, educators can promote a culture of peace and tolerance in schools and communities.

2. **Fostering Empathy and Understanding:** Conflict resolution skills encourage empathy, perspective-taking, and understanding of others' viewpoints and experiences. By learning to see conflicts from different perspectives and engage in active listening and empathy-building exercises, students develop a deeper appreciation for diversity and learn to respect and value differences among their peers.

3. **Building Positive Relationships:** Conflict resolution skills strengthen interpersonal relationships by fostering trust, communication, and cooperation among individuals. By teaching students how to express their needs and concerns assertively, listen actively to others, and collaborate on finding mutually acceptable solutions, educators can create a supportive and inclusive learning environment where students feel valued and respected.

4. **Preparing for Future Challenges:** Conflict resolution skills are essential for navigating complex social, cultural, and political issues in an increasingly interconnected and diverse world. By equipping students with the skills they need to address conflicts effectively, educators prepare them to become active and responsible global citizens capable of contributing to positive social change and building a more just and equitable society.

Teaching Conflict Resolution Skills

There are several approaches and strategies for teaching conflict resolution skills in educational settings:

1. **Social and Emotional Learning (SEL):** SEL programs integrate conflict resolution skills into the curriculum, teaching students essential competencies such as self-awareness, self-management, social awareness, relationship skills, and responsible decision-making. By embedding conflict resolution skills into everyday classroom activities and interactions, educators can promote students' social and emotional well-being and enhance their ability to navigate conflicts constructively.

2. **Peer Mediation Programs:** Peer mediation programs train students to serve as mediators and facilitators in resolving conflicts among their peers. By providing training in active listening, communication, and problem-solving techniques, peer mediators help their classmates resolve conflicts amicably and

collaboratively, reducing the need for adult intervention and empowering students to take ownership of their conflicts.

3. **Restorative Practices:** Restorative practices focus on repairing harm and restoring relationships in the aftermath of conflicts or wrongdoing. Restorative circles, conferences, and restorative justice approaches provide opportunities for dialogue, reflection, and accountability, allowing individuals involved in conflicts to express their feelings, share their perspectives, and work together to find resolutions that address the underlying causes of harm and prevent future conflicts.

4. **Conflict Resolution Workshops and Training:** Educators can facilitate conflict resolution workshops and training sessions to teach students specific skills and techniques for managing conflicts effectively. Role-playing exercises, case studies, and simulations allow students to practice communication, negotiation, and problem-solving skills in realistic scenarios, building their confidence and competence in resolving conflicts in diverse contexts.

Challenges and Considerations

Teaching conflict resolution skills in educational settings may face several challenges:

1. **Cultural and Contextual Differences:** Conflict resolution approaches may vary across cultures and contexts, requiring sensitivity to cultural norms, values, and practices. Educators must adapt conflict resolution strategies to the cultural and linguistic diversity of their students and communities, ensuring that interventions are culturally relevant and respectful of students' backgrounds and identities.

2. **Power Imbalances:** Power imbalances among students or between students and educators can complicate conflict

resolution processes and undermine their effectiveness. Educators must be mindful of power dynamics and strive to create a safe and equitable learning environment where all voices are heard and respected, and where conflicts are addressed with fairness and impartiality.

3. **Resistance to Change:** Some students or stakeholders may resist efforts to teach conflict resolution skills, viewing conflicts as inevitable or believing that aggression or avoidance is the best way to deal with conflicts. Educators must engage in ongoing dialogue and communication to overcome resistance and foster a culture of openness, collaboration, and mutual respect for conflict resolution efforts to succeed.

4. **Resource Constraints:** Limited resources, including time, funding, and training opportunities, may pose challenges to implementing comprehensive conflict resolution programs in educational settings. Educators must advocate for adequate resources and support from school administrators, policymakers, and community stakeholders to ensure the sustainability and scalability of conflict resolution initiatives.

Teaching conflict resolution skills is essential for fostering harmony, cooperation, and understanding among students and communities. By equipping students with the skills they need to manage conflicts constructively, educators can promote a culture of peace, tolerance, and respect in schools and society. By embedding conflict resolution principles and practices into the curriculum, peer mediation programs, restorative practices, and conflict resolution workshops, educators can empower students to become active agents of change capable of addressing conflicts effectively and contributing to a more just and equitable world for all.

Cultivating Empathy and Cultural Understanding in Schools

In today's increasingly diverse and interconnected world, fostering empathy and cultural understanding is essential for creating inclusive and harmonious learning environments where students feel valued, respected, and supported. Cultivating empathy—the ability to understand and share the feelings of others—and cultural understanding—the ability to appreciate and respect diverse cultures, perspectives, and experiences—is not only important for promoting positive social relationships but also for preparing students to thrive in a globalized society. This chapter explores strategies, approaches, and best practices for cultivating empathy and cultural understanding in schools, examining the benefits, challenges, and implications of fostering these essential competencies for students' academic, social, and emotional development.

Understanding Empathy and Cultural Understanding

Before delving into strategies for cultivating empathy and cultural understanding in schools, it is important to clarify what these concepts entail:

1. **Empathy:** Empathy involves the ability to understand and share the feelings, thoughts, and perspectives of others. It encompasses emotional empathy—feeling what others are feeling, cognitive empathy—understanding what others are feeling, and compassionate empathy—responding to others' feelings with kindness and compassion. Empathy enables individuals to connect with others, build meaningful relationships, and demonstrate care and concern for their well-being.

2. **Cultural Understanding:** Cultural understanding involves the ability to appreciate and respect diverse cultures, traditions,

values, and ways of life. It encompasses knowledge of cultural norms, practices, and beliefs, as well as an awareness of the historical, social, and political contexts that shape cultural identities and experiences. Cultural understanding enables individuals to navigate cross-cultural interactions, challenge stereotypes and prejudices, and embrace diversity as a source of strength and enrichment.

Strategies for Cultivating Empathy and Cultural Understanding

There are several strategies and approaches that educators can use to cultivate empathy and cultural understanding in schools:

1. **Promoting Diversity and Inclusion:** Creating a diverse and inclusive school environment is essential for fostering empathy and cultural understanding. Educators can celebrate diversity through multicultural curriculum, literature, and activities that reflect the experiences and perspectives of students from different backgrounds. By promoting respect for diversity and challenging stereotypes and biases, educators can create opportunities for students to learn from one another and develop empathy for individuals from diverse cultural, racial, ethnic, and socioeconomic backgrounds.

2. **Encouraging Perspective-Taking:** Encouraging perspective-taking activities can help students develop empathy by putting themselves in others' shoes and seeing the world from different perspectives. Role-playing exercises, literature circles, and classroom discussions allow students to explore characters' thoughts, feelings, and motivations, fostering empathy and understanding for diverse experiences and viewpoints. By encouraging empathy-building activities, educators can cultivate students' ability to empathize with others and respond with kindness and compassion.

3. **Facilitating Cross-Cultural Experiences:** Providing opportunities for cross-cultural experiences can broaden students' horizons and deepen their cultural understanding. Cultural exchange programs, field trips, and guest speakers from diverse backgrounds expose students to different cultures, traditions, and ways of life, fostering appreciation and respect for cultural diversity. By facilitating cross-cultural interactions and experiences, educators can promote empathy and cultural understanding as students learn to navigate and appreciate diverse perspectives and experiences.

4. **Encouraging Empathy through Service Learning:** Engaging students in service learning projects can cultivate empathy by providing opportunities to connect with individuals and communities in need. Service learning projects allow students to apply classroom knowledge and skills to real-world issues, fostering empathy and compassion for others' struggles and challenges. By engaging in meaningful service activities, students develop a sense of social responsibility and empathy as they work collaboratively to address community needs and make a positive difference in the world.

Benefits of Cultivating Empathy and Cultural Understanding

Cultivating empathy and cultural understanding in schools has numerous benefits for students, educators, and communities:

1. **Promotes Positive Social Relationships:** Empathy and cultural understanding are essential for building positive social relationships based on respect, trust, and mutual understanding. Students who possess empathy and cultural understanding are more likely to form meaningful connections with their peers, teachers, and community members, fostering a sense of belonging and support in the school environment.

2. **Enhances Academic Achievement:** Empathy and cultural understanding contribute to academic achievement by promoting collaboration, critical thinking, and communication skills. Students who possess empathy and cultural understanding are better equipped to work effectively in diverse teams, engage in respectful dialogue and debate, and appreciate multiple perspectives, enhancing their academic performance and success.

3. **Prepares Students for Global Citizenship:** Empathy and cultural understanding are essential competencies for global citizenship in an increasingly interconnected and diverse world. Students who possess empathy and cultural understanding are better prepared to navigate cross-cultural interactions, advocate for social justice and equity, and contribute to positive social change in their communities and beyond.

4. **Reduces Prejudice and Discrimination:** Empathy and cultural understanding help combat prejudice, stereotypes, and discrimination by fostering appreciation and respect for diversity. Students who possess empathy and cultural understanding are less likely to engage in biased attitudes and behaviors and more likely to challenge stereotypes and promote inclusivity and equity in their schools and communities.

Challenges and Considerations

Cultivating empathy and cultural understanding in schools may face several challenges:

1. **Addressing Bias and Prejudice:** Addressing bias and prejudice among students and educators is essential for fostering empathy and cultural understanding. Educators must be vigilant in challenging stereotypes and biases and creating a safe and inclusive learning environment where all students feel valued, respected, and supported.

2. **Navigating Difficult Conversations:** Navigating difficult conversations about sensitive topics such as race, ethnicity, religion, and social justice requires skill and sensitivity. Educators must be prepared to facilitate open and respectful dialogue, provide accurate information, and create opportunities for students to express their perspectives and experiences in a safe and supportive environment.

3. **Building Cultural Competence:** Building cultural competence among educators is essential for effectively promoting empathy and cultural understanding in schools. Educators must engage in ongoing professional development and self-reflection to deepen their understanding of cultural diversity and develop the skills and knowledge needed to create inclusive learning environments that celebrate diversity and promote equity and social justice.

4. **Engaging Families and Communities:** Engaging families and communities in promoting empathy and cultural understanding is essential for creating a collaborative and supportive learning environment. Educators must work closely with families and community stakeholders to build partnerships, address cultural differences and barriers to engagement, and ensure that school initiatives reflect the needs and values of diverse communities.

Cultivating empathy and cultural understanding in schools is essential for promoting positive social relationships, enhancing academic achievement, preparing students for global citizenship, and reducing prejudice and discrimination. By promoting diversity and inclusion, encouraging perspective-taking, facilitating cross-cultural experiences, and encouraging empathy through service learning, educators can create learning environments where students feel valued, respected, and supported. By addressing challenges and considerations such as bias and prejudice, difficult conversations, cultural competence, and family and community engagement, educators can foster empathy and cultural understanding in schools and empower students to become compassionate, empathetic, and culturally competent global citizens committed to building a more just, equitable, and harmonious world for all.

Promoting Global Citizenship Education

Global citizenship education (GCE) is an essential component of contemporary education, aimed at preparing students to navigate the complexities of our interconnected world and become active and responsible global citizens. GCE emphasizes the development of knowledge, skills, and attitudes that empower individuals to engage critically with global issues, appreciate cultural diversity, and take action to address social, environmental, and economic challenges. This chapter explores the importance of promoting global citizenship education in schools, examining strategies, approaches, and best practices for fostering global awareness, understanding, and engagement among students.

Understanding Global Citizenship Education

Global citizenship education encompasses a broad range of concepts and competencies, including:

1. **Global Awareness:** Global citizenship education promotes awareness of interconnectedness and interdependence among individuals, communities, and nations across the globe. It encourages students to recognize the ways in which global issues such as climate change, poverty, conflict, and migration impact people's lives and communities worldwide, fostering a sense of shared responsibility and solidarity with others.

2. **Cultural Understanding:** Global citizenship education emphasizes appreciation and respect for cultural diversity and

intercultural dialogue. It encourages students to recognize and celebrate the richness of cultural traditions, values, and perspectives around the world, fostering empathy, tolerance, and respect for differences. Cultural understanding is essential for building inclusive and harmonious societies where all individuals feel valued and respected.

3. **Critical Thinking:** Global citizenship education cultivates critical thinking skills, enabling students to analyze and evaluate complex global issues from multiple perspectives. It encourages students to question assumptions, challenge stereotypes and biases, and seek evidence-based solutions to global challenges. Critical thinking empowers students to become informed and engaged global citizens capable of understanding and addressing the root causes of social, economic, and environmental problems.

4. **Social Responsibility:** Global citizenship education promotes a sense of social responsibility and ethical engagement with global issues. It encourages students to recognize their role and agency as global citizens and take action to promote social justice, human rights, and sustainable development. Social responsibility involves advocating for positive change, supporting marginalized communities, and contributing to efforts to address global challenges at the local, national, and international levels.

Strategies for Promoting Global Citizenship Education

There are several strategies and approaches that educators can use to promote global citizenship education in schools:

1. **Integration into the Curriculum:** Integrating global citizenship education into the curriculum across subject areas enables students to explore global issues and perspectives in various contexts. Educators can incorporate global themes, case

studies, and projects into lessons and assignments, connecting classroom learning to real-world issues and promoting critical thinking and global awareness across disciplines.

2. **Experiential Learning:** Experiential learning opportunities such as service learning projects, cultural exchanges, and international partnerships provide students with hands-on experiences that deepen their understanding of global issues and foster empathy and cultural understanding. By engaging in meaningful activities and interactions with individuals and communities from diverse backgrounds, students develop the knowledge, skills, and attitudes needed to become effective global citizens.

3. **Cross-Cultural Dialogue:** Facilitating cross-cultural dialogue and exchange opportunities allows students to interact with peers from different cultural, ethnic, and socioeconomic backgrounds, fostering empathy, understanding, and respect for diversity. Educators can organize cultural events, workshops, and discussion groups that encourage students to share their perspectives, experiences, and values, creating opportunities for meaningful intercultural exchange and learning.

4. **Community Engagement:** Engaging with local and global communities enables students to connect classroom learning to real-world issues and take action to address social, environmental, and economic challenges. Educators can collaborate with community organizations, NGOs, and international agencies to develop service learning projects, advocacy campaigns, and volunteer opportunities that empower students to make a positive difference in their communities and the world.

Benefits of Promoting Global Citizenship Education

Promoting global citizenship education in schools offers numerous benefits for students, educators, and communities:

1. **Prepares Students for the Globalized World:** Global citizenship education equips students with the knowledge, skills, and attitudes they need to thrive in an interconnected and interdependent world. By fostering global awareness, cultural understanding, and critical thinking skills, GCE prepares students to navigate complex global issues and engage responsibly as citizens of the world.

2. **Promotes Inclusion and Equity:** Global citizenship education promotes inclusivity and equity by celebrating diversity and challenging inequalities and injustices. By fostering empathy, tolerance, and respect for cultural differences, GCE creates inclusive learning environments where all students feel valued, respected, and supported, regardless of their background or identity.

3. **Encourages Civic Engagement:** Global citizenship education encourages students to become active and responsible global citizens committed to social justice and sustainable development. By promoting social responsibility, ethical engagement, and advocacy skills, GCE empowers students to take action on issues that matter to them and contribute to positive social change in their communities and the world.

4. **Fosters Collaboration and Cooperation:** Global citizenship education fosters collaboration and cooperation among students, educators, and communities, enabling them to work together to address shared challenges and achieve common goals. By promoting cross-cultural dialogue, mutual understanding, and collective action, GCE builds bridges between individuals and

communities and promotes a culture of peace, tolerance, and solidarity.

Challenges and Considerations

Promoting global citizenship education in schools may face several challenges:

1. **Curricular Constraints:** Incorporating global citizenship education into the curriculum may be challenging due to time constraints, standardized testing requirements, and competing priorities. Educators must find creative ways to integrate GCE into existing courses and programs while addressing curricular constraints and ensuring alignment with educational standards and objectives.

2. **Teacher Preparation:** Educators may lack the training and resources needed to effectively teach global citizenship education. Professional development opportunities, resources, and support are essential for equipping educators with the knowledge, skills, and confidence to integrate GCE into their teaching practice and create meaningful learning experiences for students.

3. **Access and Equity:** Access to global citizenship education may be limited for some students, particularly those from marginalized or underserved communities. Ensuring equitable access to GCE requires addressing barriers such as socioeconomic disparities, language barriers, and cultural biases, and providing support and resources to enable all students to participate fully in GCE initiatives.

4. **Cultural Sensitivity:** Promoting global citizenship education requires cultural sensitivity and awareness of diverse perspectives and experiences. Educators must be mindful of cultural differences, power dynamics, and potential sources of

conflict and misunderstanding when facilitating cross-cultural dialogue and exchange, ensuring that GCE initiatives are inclusive, respectful, and culturally relevant.

Promoting global citizenship education in schools is essential for preparing students to navigate the complexities of our interconnected world and become active and responsible global citizens. By fostering global awareness, cultural understanding, critical thinking, and social responsibility, GCE equips students with the knowledge, skills, and attitudes they need to address global challenges, promote social justice, and contribute to positive social change in their communities and the world. By integrating GCE into the curriculum, providing experiential learning opportunities, facilitating cross-cultural dialogue, and engaging with local and global communities, educators can create inclusive and empowering learning environments where students develop the competencies needed to thrive as citizens of the world. Despite challenges such as curricular constraints, teacher preparation, access and equity, and cultural sensitivity, promoting global citizenship education offers numerous benefits for students, educators, and communities, paving the way for a more just, equitable, and harmonious world for all.

www.ingramcontent.com/pod-product-compliance
Lightning Source LLC
LaVergne TN
LVHW061528070526
838199LV00009B/415